Su M T W Th F S

THE INTENTIONAL WEEK

See Your Week Differently.
Live Your Life Intentionally.

By Matt Granados
Author of Multiple #1 International Bestsellers

Intentional Week

See Your Week Differently. Live Your Life Intentionally.

Copyright © 2021 by Matt Granados

RHG Media Productions
25495 Southwick Drive #103
Hayward, CA 94544.

The Courage of a Leader® is a registered trademark

ISBN 978-1-7350997-3-6 (ebook)
ISBN 978-1-7350997-4-3 (paperback)
ISBN 978-1-7350997-5-0 (hardcover)

Visit us on line at **www.YourPurposeDrivenPractice.com**

Printed in the United States of America.

FROM THE AUTHOR

Dear Reader,

I am so excited for you to take part in this journey to create intentional weeks in your life. I live by the philosophy that I rarely will change a life in a week, but if I change your weeks, I most certainly will change your life.

As you journey through this book, you will be asked to learn new things, focus on different things, and remember old things. Most importantly, you will be asked to view your weeks differently.

Each week is made up of 604,800 seconds, which is the same as 10,080 minutes, 168 hours, and 7 days.

The week is like the finish line, but the days are the path we need to take to see the finish line.

Sunday, Monday, Tuesday, Wednesday, Thursday, Friday, and Saturday.

We have developed a bit of a challenge that you can take part in while you experience this book (not just read) over the next ninety days. It is a challenge that has been attempted by people all over the world and has humbled nearly everyone who has attempted it.

We call it the i90 Challenge and it is described as such: Easy to understand, simple to do, difficult to complete.

As the author of the book, today, I have yet to be able to finish it perfectly, but I finish it every ninety days. It is a challenge about progress versus perfection. Effort versus outcome. Discipline versus everything in life that pulls at you.

So, if you are interested, since you purchased this book, you can be a part of this challenge for free.

You also are invited into our private Facebook group when you decide to take this challenge so you can connect with individuals all over the world also trying to increase intentionality in their lives.

You are not alone in wanting this, and you are not alone in seeking this.

Just go to www.LifePulseInc.com/i90 to access the challenge at no charge and to get started today as you get through this book.

Intentionally,

Matt Granados

ACKNOWLEDGMENTS

In past books, I have thanked my family, my mentors and my friends, but when it comes to whom I want to acknowledge and dedicate this book, it is you—the reader.

This is a book we developed so you can live every single day of the week with intention. This is a book we developed for you to break down, tear apart and use to get the most out of each week. This is a book we developed for you to share with others and work through the content—by yourself or as a team—and live a fulfilled and enjoyable life.

So, thank you to my mentors, my family, and my friends, but I want to acknowledge and thank *you* for taking the first step in a life-changing method. Stick with *Intentional Week*, and you'll soon be living the life you've always desired.

Thank you.

CONTENTS

INTRODUCTION

Welcome to The Intentional Week. It may seem strange that I would "welcome" you to such a thing, but what we are about to do is transform how you live life in a way that will allow you to stay fulfilled in all things of value while still working toward goals in your life while limiting the number of regrets and mistakes you make along the way. When we are not intentional, it is like we are driving on the highway and not knowing what exit we need to get off. It is like running a race with no finish line. It is like living a life that is not worth living.

The point of this book is to simply walk you through a process that we have discovered that will allow you to live each week full of intention. We have found that you will not change your life in a week, but if you change your weeks, you most definitely will change your life.

We are not going to fluff this book with feel-good lines or colorful word pictures, as we want you to get exactly what you need as fast as possible. Your time is valuable, and we want to get you started on this right away.

As we get started on how to create intentional weeks in your life, I want you to get started on two simple tasks each morning that will dramatically impact your day. Start both of them today, and if you have not done one, as soon as you are home, do the second suggested daily action. Both start in the morning and one takes literally no time (just a decision), and the second takes less than five minutes.

Both of these things are simple, easy, and anyone can do them. They are things we all probably used to do at some point but have gotten away from them. These will also seem insignificant but try it and experience how much better your day begins and ends. It is incredible.

Make the decision right now that you do not use your snooze button on your alarm.

Make your bed every morning as part of your morning routine.

Both of these are simple, easy, and anyone can do them. They *are* things we all have done and one point in our lives, but we have not given any value to them. These will start your days as intentional and in order.

Now that your bed is made let's jump into how to build out your weeks.

First, let me explain one thing. If you get *nothing* else from this book, this will open your eyes as to why we are so passionate about the systems we teach and the value of focusing on intentional weeks.

We have been working with individuals all over the planet in industries of all kinds, and here is the biggest thing we realized. Using our systems does not take a lot of time for the user to get the results we are looking to get. So much so that we offer a money-back guarantee on one of our coaching programs, which is basically unheard of in this industry. We are so confident in our systems that if we do not hit the goals we set with clients using the plan we create, we give them their money back!

The reason we can do this is that we understand and leverage the value of a week. What we have also found that no matter what position the client holds, CEO or an entry-level employee when people follow our system, it takes anywhere from ten to sixteen hours a week to live a fulfilled life and achieve the goals they set.

Let me explain what that means. We put this at the end of *every* plan we create for our clients. This is how the time of the week breaks down to hours.

Time in a week: 168 hours a week

- Sleep 8 hours a day - 56 hours a week, leaving 112 hours.
- Eat 3 hours a day (3 meals) - 21 hours a week, leaving 91 hours.
- Work 8–12 hours a day - 40–60 hours a week, leaving 31–51 hours.

What are you doing with the 30–50 extra hours a week?

You do not have a time issue.

You have a spending issue.

Let me explain who I am and what our company does. My name is Matt Granados, and before we were married, my wife Maria came to me and said something profound. I will paraphrase a bit, but here was our conversation:

MARIA: Matt, I love you. But . . . (which we know is not going to go well) I knew being with you would be hard, but I never thought it would be *this* hard. You're crazy. How do you manage all that chaos in your head for the week?

MATT: I have a couple of questions I ask myself at the beginning of the week, and that's how I know how to spend my time.

MARIA: Could we talk about them together?

MATT: Sure, here they are!

MARIA: These are good but let's put them in a book and make it actually look nice!

Like the nerds that we are, Maria took these nine questions that I used to set up my week and created the first version of the LP Planner.

Now, at the time, this was just for us to use, but when others asked if they could get a copy, we started giving them out to people. Eventually, a large financial institution contacted us and said our system solves their biggest personnel problem. They wanted to know if we could help.

That is when Life Pulse, Inc. was created. We didn't know this system would do what it has been able to do in companies ranging from Twitter to Google's headquarters to the United States Air Force. We knew it helped us, but we had no clue that it would help thousands of people all over the world. I would love to say we had the vision of how to build this consulting company from the beginning. In reality, Life Pulse was created not because we wanted it, but because others needed a system to help bring intentionality back to life.

That is what we do. That is what this system does. That is exactly what this book will do for you if you let it.

THE VALUE OF THE EXPERIENCE

Over the years, we have discovered what we call the LP Structure of Success. We had to breakdown what it is we do each day, week, month, and quarter. We have plenty of exercises we do with clients, such as annual retreats and a fifteen-year vision, which you can access on our website, but for the sake of the intentional week and to get you the result ASAP, we are not going to go into them in this book.

Let's take a second and understand this LP Structure of Success, for if you live by this, in all areas of your life, using our books and tools or not, you will live a life of intentionality:

Daily Actions: Once we plan, then it is time to act on it. Never try to plan and execute at the same time. According to our time working with Navy SEAL trainers, this is how people get hurt (or get nothing done).

Weekly Planning: This is how we plan our life. One week at a time.

Monthly Celebration: Taking time each month to review what has happened and celebrate life (you may have heard us call it a Life Date).

Quarterly Review: As you would in any health business, taking time to look back on the quarter as a whole and evaluate your actions, plans, and celebrations. At this point, we can reset and see what we are doing next in our life.

How It Will Work

Everything we teach or coach on at Life Pulse is based on ninety-day cycles. Ninety days/three months/one quarter has been shown to us as the best way to set goals, follow through with goals, and achieve goals. Also, the key to successfully implementing something is through repetition. The final key to allow a system to stick as part of your life is simultaneously learning and doing at the same time. We want to give you a solution for all three in this program.

We will breakdown some of our most effective principles we have discovered through working successfully with clients all over the world. I would ask that you take the *very* short time it takes and read the intro chapters and the breakdown of what we will be doing each week. You do not need to go into what we want you to read about each day, but if you are an overachiever, go for the whole book, from front to back. This way, you fully understand what we are doing, where we are going, and how we are getting there.

Once you have gotten these principles understood, we can get started on the work. If for some reason, you just want to get into the work, the system will work for you, but it will be a bit more challenging for you to keep focused and disciplined, but hey, this is your week. You got this book because you want it to be intentional. Your choices are what will or will not make this work, as it has for many in the past.

We have set up a four-week process, which will be cycled each month. Because of how we know repetition is key and learning while doing is helpful, you will be going through the four-week cycle three separate times. However, I ask each week, once you feel you have mastered the first step, you can go to the next. Some people spend all ninety days just on the first step, and others seem to get all three in the ninety days. For the first cycle, you will be in the mindset of the Mentee to me, then as a Peer to me, and finally as a Mentor to me. That is right; you will go through this as the student who will quickly become the teacher. As you go through the program, depending on which cycle you are in, this is where your mindset should be:

- **Mentee:** This is when I am telling you what to do and why to do it, and you are to do it how I teach it.
- **Peer:** This is when I am telling you what to do and why to do it, and you are to do it how *you* feel it needs to be done in your life.
- **Mentor:** This is when I am telling you what to do and why to do it, and you are to do it so you can teach someone else how to do it.

If it sounds strange that you will be repeating the same things multiple times, it can only mean that you haven't experienced how simple life can be lived when proper systems are implemented. We are all creatures of habit. You have routines that, when you do not do, make you feel "off." Everything we do and teach is to make creating these routines simple, easy, and most importantly, effective.

Life is not supposed to be hard. Books like these are not supposed to be confusing. Simplicity is the key, and systems are what makes simplicity also effective. We have been told our whole life we need to work hard, and if we don't feel it, then it is not working. A mentor once told me that making money is fun but making a lot of money—well, that becomes boring. When I was young and first starting out, I could not wrap my head around it. I feel making money would be fun, but why would it be boring to make a lot of money? The reason is to make a couple hundred thousand a year is challenging, but in order to make more than that consistently, it takes implementing proper systems in your life that consistently are implemented and gaining a compound effect on the actions you previously took. It is not about working hard; it is about finding systems that help life be more fulfilled and each week be more intentional.

Remember, this is not a race to the finish line but a chance for you to stride with confidence through an intentional and fulfilled life! Remember, you will not change your life in a week, but if you change the weeks in your life, no matter where you are, you can get where you want to be.

THE VALUE OF THE WEEK

What is so good about this seven-day period that we call a week? It has been the biggest game-changer when it has come to planning that I have experience for myself and my clients. If you have ever read anything about planning, you may have heard about a weekly planner, but rarely are you told about why the week is so powerful. Before we get into the week, we need to discuss the measurements of time that precede the week. Now, we do not have dates when each was recognized by humans, but I feel humans recognized days, then years, then months, just based on what happens at the beginning/end of each cycle.

See, primitive people did not need time as we do to schedule our summer vacations or what we are doing for the weekend. Instead, they needed to pay attention to these cycles in order to survive and thrive. For example, they only could measure days (the space between nights), years (the space between leaves growing on trees), and then months (the space between moons). Just think about what it must have been like to be outside and experience things like the new day. Notice that leaves and grass are starting to grow again after so long, or looking up, and the positioning of the moon has changed, but then went back to where it started. The feeling of mystical fear is all I can think of with a burning desire to bring reason to this obvious cycle. These cycles were essential in order to be able to evolve practices, so we can make the most of what nature offers in the timeframe nature offers it to us.

Okay, so day, year, and month make sense to me, but why a week? In doing research on why there are seven days in a week, all I could understand is it is one of two sources.

The first is from the biblical story of creation. The seventh day was the Sabbath, and due to Jewish laws at the time. The Sabbath naturally feels like the end of a week, as no work was allowed but was used for rest and worship. Remember, at this time, religion was intertwined, and in some places, was the law of society.

The second, and in my opinion, more likely, source was the Roman Empire. Highly influenced by the two main religions at the time, Judaism and the newer religion of Christianity, it is not a surprise this similar structure was adopted.

The crazy thing is we live our weeks as if it is a natural cycle, and it turns out (unless it is divinely connected to creationism, which there is no known proof it is) the measurement of a week is an entirely artificial period of time. When it comes to survival in a primitive nature, a week has no purpose. But we do not live in that time. Right now, we live in a globalized society where we need some order of time that was not needed prior. Times have changed. Days are important, years are important, and months are important, but what is the value of the week? The most likely reason for the creation of the week was because commerce benefits from regularity.

It turns out we also benefit from the regularity. When I ask people if they plan their life, if they are above average, they may set goals once a year and a daily to-do list. The problem is a to-do list helps you not forget things but does nothing (and sometimes hurts) to your ability to be efficient, and more importantly, intentional.

I am here to tell you that your life will not be changed in a week, but if you start being intentional each week, your life will be changed. We have found that the week has two direct benefits. The first is the fact that it seems to be the perfect measurement of time. A day is too short, and a month is too long, but if we were to ask Goldilocks, a week is just *perfect*. A week gives the flexibility we need for life with the urgency we need to act.

If you are living your life day by day, you are going to constantly be playing catch-up, and you will most likely be very reactive toward what life throws your way. Also, within a twenty-four-hour period, it is *very* easy for an emergency to come up and throw you off track. Because it is such a short period of time, it is nearly impossible to get back on track on that same day. Think about your life and when you have been thrown off, as I am saying. It is as if we put our arms up and throw in the towel on the day. We tell ourselves that we will get it tomorrow, and we both know there is a *high* likelihood that the task will also not get done tomorrow. Living a day at a time is like closing your eyes in the middle of a cornfield, spinning around, and then opening your eyes to walk and find exactly where you want to be. This is the ultimate plan if you feel like wandering through life and ending up wherever life takes you.

Some people like to plan out their month, which there is some benefit in doing that, but we found if your goals are only going to take a month to do, they may be more of a task than a goal! Let's raise that bar and get more out of life. Triple these monthly tasks that you are calling goals and create your quarterly goals. But back to planning monthly. Now, this does solve the problem of day-to-day planning, of which there is not enough margin in case of life "happening," but the issue is there is *no* urgency. This was like when we were back in school, and we had a project to get done. Even with all the intentions in the world, if we have a month to do something, we will wait till the last minute to get it done. It is as if procrastination is in our DNA as humans with how natural it feels.

So again, and I will repeat myself because it is *so* important. A day is too short, and a month is too long. A week is perfect because it gives you the margin/flexibility a day does not with urgency, and compared to a month, a week gives you the urgency while still allowing the flexibility/margin needed. When we describe a week to our clients, we want you to think of it as linear, meaning if you cannot do something on Monday, depending on the task, you can move it to Tuesday. Then, if Tuesday gets thrown off, you can move some of Tuesday's things to Wednesday, and so on. This gives us the ability to live life while still being intentional in what we do. If we need to change a day, instead of not getting to it, we will move it to another day.

This is why we do everything based on a term we use called "Time Chunks" and "Time Buckets."

Time Chunks: Small amounts of time, no more than ninety minutes, that you can set to focus on a specific task. (Spend sixty minutes researching a prospect, cleaning the backyard, playing with your kids, reading a book, going to the gym.)

Time Buckets: Specific amount of time, usually no more than three hours at a time, where you will set aside for categories of tasks. (On Tuesday and Thursday from 9:00 a.m. to 12:00 noon, I work on growing my business, maintenance on my business, following up with coworkers/employees/clients, working toward specific projects, doing family time, house projects, working on self-growth, working on self-maintenance.)

The reason I love to do Time Chunks is that if I have three separate Time Chunks on Monday and an emergency pops up, I can take that Time Chuck and move it to Tuesday or later in the week. I just need to make sure I get my goals done.

The biggest benefit of Time Buckets is it gives me a place to put certain tasks. For example, if a client calls me and wants to talk about new services through LP, I can look at my week and find the Time Bucket that is designated for growing my business. In the example, it is Tuesday from 9–12 noon, so that is where I am going to try to schedule this call. If that doesn't work, how about Thursday from 9–noon? If they cannot do those two times, then maybe we need to wait until next week. Some of you are cringing at the thought that I would make a prospect wait a week versus close right there. My first response to you is how desperate are you, but my second and more loving response is we have a solution for that.

In the case that is a *big* opportunity, and you do not want to miss it, you should try to find a way to move that three-hour Time Bucket to another time that works for them. Sometimes I have to break up my Time Buckets.

The key of these Time Buckets or Time Chunks is we are consciously setting time to dedicate to the tasks that need to be done. I do not care if the three hours actually happens on Tuesday at 9:00 a.m. or spread out throughout the week, but the goal is to make sure the three hours happen. Otherwise, you have a high likelihood of never getting in what is needed.

These Time Chunks and Time Buckets also save you from spending too much time on tasks that do not need your time and attention at this moment. When we are creating content, I can do it for hours. I *love* doing it, but in order to live a fulfilled and intentional life, I need to be able to focus on all parts of life that need my attention. We can also go back to what we want to do once everything else is taken care of. This is why the structure of an intentional wheel is simple but specific.

Again, a reminder of what I wrote in the Introduction to ask you what you are doing the 168 hours of the week we get every seven days.

We have worked with individuals all over the planet in industries of all kinds, and here is the biggest thing we realized: it does not take a lot of time to do what we are looking to do.

The reason we can do this is that we get the value of a week. What we have also found that no matter who the client is. No matter if they are the CEO or an entry-level employee, when people follow our system, to live a fulfilled life and achieve the goals we say we want on a weekly basis usually takes about no more than 10 hours a week for personal goals and no more than 10 hours a week for Professional Goals.

THE VALUE OF THE STRUCTURE

I will *always* suggest you plan your week before it starts. Most of our LP users do this on Sunday, as it is the day we feel ends the week. *Please* do not try to do it Monday morning! This is a receipt for disaster. If you currently get stressed thinking about work, then I have suggested to other clients to do this Friday before you leave work for the day or before you get home. Using the LP, this process takes about twenty minutes when you get used to it. I tell people to give themselves thirty to sixty minutes when they first get started so it can be a relaxing experience as you are figuring it out. Rushing yourself while trying to learn will lead you to get discouraged and probably discontinuing the process. No matter what day you choose to do it, just make sure you are doing the planning before the start of your week.

On Sunday, we will ask nine specific questions, which are what created the LP system and will allow you to naturally use Reverse Planning (explained in a later chapter). If you want to skip that, you can, but to see the full results of what we are doing, you will want to make sure you are getting your mind in the right direction before you start planning. Otherwise, you're just throwing darts in the dark, hoping to hit the board, let alone a bullseye.

So assuming you've done something to get your mindset right, I use the five days of the workweek differently, and I also use certain times of the day the best I can. I do this so I can suggest times that make sense based on this structure. Here are a couple of things I try to do. First, I try to do as many creative work/growth tasks before noon each day. This way, they are uninterrupted by something new that day, and it allows others to collaborate or take action before the end of their workday. After noon, I like to use this time for as many meetings or tasks related to operations or maintenance. This way, I am not distracted, I can take necessary actions

before noon:
- creative/growth tasks

after noon:
ops + maintenance + meetings

23

before the work is done, but also I can sleep on major problems versus letting them completely disrupt my day.

Here is the caveat. This is how I structure my week, but this does not mean this is how my week is going to go. There are a lot of moving parts in life that will force me to change this, but it gives me a fighting chance to be able to get done what I want and need without getting pulled by others, issues, and life in general.

So here is what each day means to me, and I would suggest you use this to get the intentional week we discussed.

Warning: Tasks are not goals. The difference is a task is a single action, whereas a goal may have multiple actions needed. I also say that a task should be able to be written in three words or less.

Monday: Heavily loaded with tasks. I will take the weekly Time Chunks I want to dedicate to tasks and make sure I use Monday to give the time each task needs. I have few meetings on Monday and few Time Buckets set if I can avoid it, but once the day starts and the show goes live, we have to be able to adapt.

Tuesday: Second heaviest day of tasks to be complete. This is where I incorporate Time Buckets with my Time Chunks. I will also try to schedule as many growth-related tasks on Tuesday so they can be put into practice and start seeing the results this week. As the day starts, we have to be able to adapt.

Wednesday: It is Hump Day. I like to take a quick ten minutes to review my weekly plan and adjust it as needed to finish the week strong. As the day starts, we have to be able to adapt. Most of the big things for the week should have been addressed on Monday or Tuesday, but the biggest part of Wednesday is what we call the Weekly Re-Group.

Thursday: Treat Thursday as the last day of my work week. Still accomplishing tasks as needed, but avoiding growth-oriented meetings/tasks/calls and making sure all maintenance is done. As the day starts, we have to be able to adapt.

Friday: Catch-up day. I block off Friday from any meetings unless there are no other options. We live by the 80/20 principle of planning. With five days in the workweek, I need to make sure I get as much as I can plan done in the 80 percent (Monday through Thursday), then I use Friday as margin to take into account the 20 percent that has thrown me off. Also, I will do almost anything I can to *never* have a new prospect or sales call on a Friday. If I am selling, I want to make sure that the prospect can take action or sleep on it for a night if needed. But if I sell on Friday, they are just trying to get to the weekend. I will push especially the most attractive sales call to Monday if I can and if I am not afraid of someone else truly taking the sale from me. Fridays are for catching up, and most importantly, they set me up for a *great weekend*!

Saturdays: Stop doing and start being. We need to value this time off, and the way I find we can do this best is to make sure what is important is done before the weekend. This is your day of rest. This is your day to just be and stop working. You can afford to take this time off, and in fact, as a human, you cannot afford to not. Sundays also will give you some time to rest unless you are planning the next week.

You know what your week is going to look like before you even start. We are able to predict the things that will throw us off this week, as they did the weeks prior. You know that if you were to be a bit more strategic about how you approached your weeks, you would experience differently and likely see better results.

So, let's start leveraging the week to get out of it everything we need to experience the best life we can imagine for ourselves and those who interact with us.

THE VALUE OF THE PLANNING

As I described the week in the previous section, I see the week as linear. Meaning, if I cannot do something on Monday, I can pass it to Tuesday. Please understand when we have this margin, we need to consciously recognize that we need to take action each day. Yes, we can push it off to tomorrow if it is not an urgent task, but if it is something that has to get done, if it is not urgent now if you push it off enough, it will become urgent.

This is why we showed how to frontload your week to make sure you are doing as much as you can in the beginning and then hopefully coasting (or choosing what you do) into the weekend. **The key to this all working is two parts. The first is planning your weeks. What this does is allows you to see the whole picture of what needs to get done in the six days between the days you plan.**

The second is the most valuable thing I do on a daily basis, and it only takes five to ten minutes *max*! We call this Planning Tomorrow Today (PTT). This is something that is not a new concept, but the value of this simple act is what allows me to make the most out of each day.

One of our clients who has used our system has stated multiple times that what he loves most about what we do is we separate planning and execution. From an average person, that would be a clever line, but this individual trains SEAL Team Six. He said the reason the SEALs do so well is that they spend the majority of their time planning so they can spend as much of a minority of their time executing. The only time there are issues in an elite team like this is when they are trying to plan when it is time to execute and vice versa.

The average person reading the book is not doing what Special Ops officers are doing but instead trying to get a better grasp on what we are doing each day. So here is what we do. Since we already have our plan of what needs to get done this week, we then look at that list and decide what we need to do.

We do this by numbering our tasks and then putting them on a structure we call our Event Manager. We call it our event manager because an event is the most basic measurement of time. Events can range from instant to a lot of time, but one thing we cannot manage is time. This is why I always tell people the concept of time management is a myth. The reason is that we cannot change time (at least not yet), and because of that, not only is there no need to manage it, but there is nothing that can be managed. From here on out, if we want to talk in terms of time management, we need to make sure we are calling it Event Management.

 Again, we call this our Event Manager, which is a modified version of a more commonly known practice called the Eisenhower Box. This was used by Dwight Eisenhower as both general and president of the United States. He would use it to delegate which tasks he would—and, even more importantly, which tasks he would not—do (delegate to someone else).

His structure was based on urgency and importance and was usually done over a large chunk of time. Ours is based on urgency and relation to our goals and is done for each day. Again, using our LP system, since you have already planned your week, this takes very little time.

 So, the box looks like this, and we use one for each day.

Eisenhower Box	Urgent	Not Urgent
Related to a goal	**Task has to happen today and is goal-oriented.** *Strategy: Do "it" immediately*	**Task can happen tomorrow and is goal-oriented.** *Strategy: Decide when you will do "it"*
Not related to a goal	**Task has to happen today and is not goal-oriented.** *Strategy: Delegate "it" to someone else*	**Task can happen tomorrow and is not goal-oriented.** *Strategy: Do "it" later*

Each day, I go through this process of PTT where I look at all of my tasks on my "Brain Dump" (list of tasks for the week), and I start to put them in order of what I'm going to get done. This Brain Dump concept is similar to how we do a puzzle. You've never done a puzzle without taking it out of the box.

So, like a puzzle, we want to get everything out of our heads and onto the table (or piece of paper). Once we have everything laid out in front of us, we can then start putting the puzzle together. This is what we do each night before the next day starts. Looking at your Brain Dump, I go through each task, taking the number for each task and deciding what box it needs to go in.

Through working with thousands of individuals throughout the years, we have seen that no matter how successful an individual is, most people are only able to effectively handle no more than seven meaningful tasks a day. When I first share that with an audience or attendees of our workshops, they laugh a bit under their breath. I can feel them thinking they have way more than seven things they need to do each day. For some, that may be true, but for most, that is not.

We feel like we have so much to do because we are holding it all in our heads. I constantly have to remind clients of our 80/20 principle that we need to control the 80 percent we can plan so the 20 percent we cannot does not overwhelm us. Although our brain is one of the most complex and impressive "computers" ever seen or experienced by man, the conscious side of the brain is pretty simple and clear. We are constantly stimulated throughout our day that we feel we can process as much as we take in. Our brain, to conserve energy, filters what we focus on from a conscious state.

So, when I was working with some military groups, I was introduced to a survival specialist. I asked him how he would suggest a civilian survive the day. After some jokes back and forth, the message I took from him was we would **take the time we waste complaining and worrying and put it toward planning and executing.**

But when I asked him how to survive if lost in the wilderness:

Me: So, what do you suggest we do if I am lost in the wilderness?

Him: There are four things you do. 1. Shelter. 2. Water. 3. Food. In that order!

Me: Sorry, but I thought you said there were four things I need to find.

Him: Not find; do. The fourth thing is to get comfy! Stay where you are unless it is dangerous because there is a better chance the military finds you than you find them.

So this really hit home with me because I like to take life experiences and use them when it comes to my intentional week. This is where our definition of wisdom comes into play:

> *Wisdom is using the correct knowledge in*
> *the correct way at the correct time.*

This is a definition we will work with that you will experience when we go through our training to build your intentional week. So here is what we need to do. Using our LP system, you will use the Event Manager that we discussed prior to determining each tasks' relationship between urgency and relation to goals. Most days, when we do this, we actually have less than seven tasks that need to be done that are urgent and related to our goals, but no matter how many tasks we must complete or what system you are using, here is how we select which seven tasks we want to take action.

This is where Survival Shapes come into play. Whether this is the first book of ours you are reading, or if you have been using our LP for years now, you will understand we try to make our techniques as simple as possible. So let's use the three shapes we first learn as kids: circles, squares, and triangles.

As we take our thoughts out of our head and put them onto paper, then we put the tasks where they belong according to relation to your goal and the urgency of the task. Remember, they are to be *tasks*, not goals. The difference is a task is a single action where a goal may have multiple actions needed. So now we can see a clear picture of the value of each task based on the day. But some days may seem like they have more for you to do than others. So this is where we need to start selecting what to do first.

So looking at today, you have a list of one to whatever number of things that you need to do. No matter how many things you have on your list, the goal is not to get *everything* done, but it is to get *the right* things done. The Survival Shapes will help us see this. To use the Survival Shapes, you get the following in your "Intentional Toolkit":

1 **Circle** (no matter what)
3 **Squares** (get it done)
3 **Triangles** (as time permits)

When we make lists, we tend to cherry-pick them based on what we want to do or what might be the easiest to do. That keeps us treading water, but that does not help us get more done with less stress. Because of this, I have already listed what was urgent and what was related to my goal, and now I get to take the seven tasks that I want to complete tomorrow and start prioritizing them.

To get really good at making the most out of the time that we have and living a life of intentionality, the ability to know what to say yes and no to is imperative. The use of Intentional Procrastination or Intentionally Stacking tasks are two key tools to this Intentional Tool Box when we are working through days that are too short to get all we need to be done.

The first tool is Intentional Procrastination, which is simple and exactly what it sounds like. It is for when we choose to delay action. I have *no* problem when clients do not do a task on purpose. Meaning they intentionally decided to hold off on doing it. Where I see people get into trouble is when they do not say *no* to anything. They then do most things at half efficiency, or they make mistakes due to being rushed. To be intentional, we need to be comfortable saying, "I'll get to that," and have the confidence that our system will help us actually get to it.

The second concept is Intentional Stacking. This is a bit more complex because there is some strategy behind it. The purpose of Intentional Stacking is so you can use the time to your advantage. Some tasks take time, so we need to take that into consideration when choosing our survival shapes. A simple one would be doing laundry at home. If it needs to get done today, it may be easier to stack it with other tasks.

There are some tasks that have a benefit for doing before others in the day. For example, if you are looking to get a response from someone, those messages may not be *as* urgent, but you may want to get those out first thing so the others can be working on getting you the answers you need while you are working on getting closer to your goals. This is Intentional Stacking, meaning you are being intentional on how you are going to get a task off your plate and onto someone else's (waiting for them to respond) while you work on the next goal you are working on. Sometimes, if my day gets away, I will schedule my email the night before to be sent the following morning so that whoever gets what I need is in work mode and ready to respond, hopefully getting me a faster response. If we are sending emails and messages at 5:00 p.m. or later, they are not responding until tomorrow anyway; we would like to be the first thing in their inbox as they start their day.

So, to do all of this in your head, as I said before, is like doing a puzzle without taking it out of the box. So without a system, this would be nearly impossible for any human to do each day properly. So let me walk you through the steps to use the tools we just introduced to you when it comes to organizing your tasks for the day. You have already used the Brain Dump to get all of your tasks/thoughts/goals out of your head and onto paper.

1. **Using the Event Manager,** determine each task's relationship with urgency (needing to be done that day) and relationship to a goal of yours.
2. **Using Intentional Procrastination,** make sure any task that does not *have* to happen that day is properly marked as not urgent.
3. **Using Intentional Stacking,** find any tasks that would benefit from happening earlier in the day than others or tasks that you need input from others (i.e., proposal, agreement, questions, etc.); make sure they are scheduled to be done when they will yield optimal benefit.
4. **Using Survival Shapes,** circle the one task (can be scheduled or not scheduled) that has to be done NMW (no matter what), then put a Square around the next three tasks to remind yourself to GID (get it done), then put a Triangle around the tasks you are going to do ATP (as time permits).

At this time, you should have your day laid out with scheduled tasks listed and the seven things that you are going to work on that day. This is where you stop focusing on the plan and start focusing on the execution. It is now time to start your day with a clear direction and simple marching orders:

your scheduled tasks, along with your Circle, three Squares, and then your three Triangles.

Once you have done this, as the survival specialist taught me, the fourth thing you do, once you have the other three elements needed for survival, is to get comfortable. If you wanted, you could move on to some other tasks on your event manager that may not have been so urgent. You can spend a bit more time on some creative tasks that you usually gave to rush. Or, and this is going to be strange for most of you reading this, this is when you can comfortably say your day is done. In today's world, the most common complaint clients and their teams have is that they cannot disconnect. That is because they start repeating the same race, day in and day out, but for some reason, they do not have a finish line. It is impossible to ever complete a race if there is no finish line. **When you complete the seven tasks, you have completed the day**. This is your finish line!

THE VALUE OF THE CHOICE

Life is not as easy as we may want it to be, but life is *much* fairer than we tend to give it credit. That is a big statement because if you have lived long enough, you have experienced something that you feel is not fair. I am not here to argue if your opinion that outcome's fairness is right or wrong because it is neither; it is your opinion, and it doesn't have to be right or wrong to be real.

But let's take a step back and think about *all* of the things that have happened in our life that we might, on the surface, say are just not fair. If we are to take our emotions out of it, look at it objectively, we can see actions, decisions, and choices we made throughout our journey that we could attribute to the suffering we may be feeling right now.

Like in the game Monopoly, life is full of chance, which we need to understand is the *very* real impact of chance in our lives is determined by the choices we make building up to that event.

Let's look at some of the many things we have a choice around that we tend to hear from clients as "out of my hands."

> We choose to understand others or disregard others' opinions.
> We choose to be offended by others or not allow them to affect us.
> We choose to be joyful or miserable.
> We choose to be fair or unfair.
> We choose to be honest or untrustworthy.
> We choose to be good or bad.

And the list can go on, but I want to jump to some of the "we choose to" statements that relate back to living out our intentional week, which leads to an intentional life.

We choose to stay focused or get distracted.
We choose to follow through or give up.
We choose to be disciplined or undisciplined.
We choose to first try and prove things right or first try to prove things wrong.
We choose to be organized or disorganized.
We choose to be efficient or wasteful.
We choose to be intentional or drift.

Choice versus condition is something we make sure all clients understand when dealing with issues. Rarely is an issue we are dealing with 100 percent conditioned-based. As I am writing this book, we are experiencing a pandemic, unlike anything our current world has ever faced. It has basically shut down the world in a matter of weeks. That is a condition that the average person could not control what happened, but the clients who were able to best handle this near-instant change were the ones who were able to best handle (and, in some cases, thrive) were the ones who made proper choices prior to the event happening.

So let's start giving value to this concept of choice versus assuming everything is by chance. Because we know what chance can do to our life, it is clear the value of choice is immense. No matter if you feel you are, we have to live with our choices no matter if they are good, so let's set ourselves up for good instead of constantly reacting a wend recovering from the bad.

THE VALUE OF THE FLOW

Before we start this chapter, do this!

Grab a new clean piece of paper (or your LP planner if you have it), and I want you to write out all of the things that you need to do for this week. If you are reading this at the end of the week, feel free to list everything you had to do this past week.

Just make that list and write out *everything*! Then set that list aside and continue reading.

What would you say if I told you that the way you have been taught to plan is detrimental to the fulfillment of your life? We have been told to make lists, use a calendar, get an app that will send you a reminder to do the task. All of these are helpful, but there is one big thing that we need to pay attention to.

We need to be aware of who we are as an individual, what we want to get out of life, and even more importantly, what is our purpose of being on this planet. Our natural mind does not take this into consideration, as the goal of our brain is to manage the body. In doing this, it is constantly trying to conserve energy. Because of that, your subconscious mind will do all that it can to make sure that *you* just do enough to survive. That is basically its job.

So we talk about how powerful the subconscious mind is, and that is very true. The majority of your brain is your subconscious mind. What we are looking to do is to train our subconscious mind; however, in order to train the subconscious mind, we need to tame the conscious mind. There are two ways to do this. First, the traditional model of "self-growth" is through force. Just stay disciplined and just take the actions. Make a choice and just do. This is *highly* effective when done but is very difficult to do. This style used to work well for me when I was young, single, and had the freedom to do anything I wanted whenever I wanted. Then life became a bit more real.

I grew up a bit; now, I have a business with employees all over the country I was responsible for. Then I decided to get married, which now gives me a new responsibility. Because I *love* being married, we decided to have kids. With kids, we needed a place to live, so we decided to buy a house. Then we decided to start some more businesses, do some physical challenges, and be an active member of the community. When life starts to get a bit more dynamic and demanding because of the responsibilities we start to have toward others, the "shut up and just do it" model does not tend to work as well. Again, it is effective, but it is not sustainable for most people.

Everything we teach needed to do three things in this order. First, be highly effective. Second, have a positive ROI on time invested. Third, be sustainable.

Like I said before, the way you were taught to plan is detrimental to the fulfillment you will experience in your life. If you want to experience this, which we do when we teach our workshops, take out a piece of paper and go through these questions. Now, try your best to only answer one at a time and not look at the next one.

Write down what you want out of this year. Make a list as extensive as you can, and have fun with it. Have it be realistic, but if you could get *everything* you want out of the next 365 days, what would that list look like?

There was a time that I call my Heart Beat, which was the lowest point of my life at that time. To simplify it, in about thirty days, I lost everything that I felt I worked so hard for. Embezzlement of my company, warning on early death, lack of internal growth and my fiancé at the time called things off right before a trip to Greece. What I realized through this experience was that my life was completely out of whack. I was focusing on just one of the four vital signs of fulfillment (professional), and when I found out about the embezzlement, that was the final straw that broke the blinders for me and forced me to see how in shambles my life was.

Explanation of **The 4 Vital Signs of Fulfillment**:

- **Internal (I)**: How are you going to grow your mind/soul/spirit?
- **Relational (R)**: How are you going to grow your connections?
- **Physical (Ph)**: How are you going to grow your body?
- **Professional (Pr)**: How are you going to grow your career?

Take the list you just wrote of *all* of the things you want this year, and I want you to put a letter corresponding to the four vital signs. If you are like most people, it is normal that you do not have all of these represented, so if you do not, just add one in the area you are missing. This also will answer a question I ask all clients, "Are your 'wants' as balanced as you want?" making sure that our wants are balanced in a way today so that we can experience the life we want to live later. If we have all of our "wants" to be in just one of these four vital signs, the other three will get ignored, and regret will find a comfortable place to live throughout your life.

Now that we have at least one thing in each of the Four Vital Signs of Fulfillment let's select one in each that we can take action on this week (or we could have taken action on last week if you are doing this exercise for this past week).

Think of one *simple* action step (Action-Based Goal) you can take during this week we are focusing on to get you a bit closer to the larger Result-Based Goal you had on your "wish list."

So you have now figured out some weekly goals you would like to focus on. Suppose you would focus on these goals, even in this small action, every week, fifty-two weeks a year. Can you imagine the progress you would see over the year? Exciting!

Now, let's compare how our flow works versus the way you likely have been taught to plan.

Average planning starts with making a list of what needs to do be done. That is what you did (hopefully). If you followed the instructions of this chapter, you have your to-do list (Brain Dump, as we call it). I want you to take a second and look at your Brain Dump (to-do list) and compare it to what actions you said you would have liked to do in your Four Vital Signs of Fulfillment.

What do you see?

Now everyone sees different things, but the majority of people see some issues with what it is they are spending their time on and what it is they say they want to be spending their time on.

I did this one time with a client, and the CEO, a very strong and powerful woman, broke down in tears when I asked this question. This was *early* in my career of speaking and teaching, so I tried to avoid bringing attention to her, but she asked if she could share something.

She explained how she has always had strong ambitions to be spiritually connected, a mother and wife who was always available for her family, healthy to fully experience life, and a beacon of light for her employees that work for her. When she looked at her Brain Dump and compared it to her weekly goals according to the Four Vital Signs of Fulfillment, she realized she was living a life most would be jealous of on paper, but internally, she was miserable and lost because she was not doing *anything* that leads to fulfillment. None of the tasks that she was doing, we connected to what she described as a fulfilled life. She was making money and considered very successful, but she was missing living a life that was fulfilling for her.

This is what we want you to start to live by. A new way of planning. A new flow of how we plan. We call it Reverse Planning.

Normally we make a list and just go through and do what we can—no endpoint. No finish. Just go, go, go. This will not lead you to fulfillment. You might luck into it, but luck is a short-term event when success is an ongoing journey.

Here is how you Reverse Plan:

First, you list everything you want to do by answering the following three questions:

What is your one-word focus for this week?
What are you grateful for this week?
What are your goals in all Four Vital Signs of Fulfillment?

Second, you list what you "need" to get done.

What is your to-do list that we call your Brain Dump?

Third, you *only* do what is important.

Using the Event Managers, we explained in "The Value of Planning" to make sure we are focusing on what is important. When we say important, that is in relation to your goals.

We ask that you *always* use Reverse Planning from here on out. This does not say just do whatever you want and forget about your other responsibilities. Instead, we want to make sure we are consciously thinking of what we need to do in order to live a fulfilled life and make sure we carve out time to do this. We suggest using the Time Chunks and Time Buckets we discussed in the "The Value of Structure" chapter so you can make sure you give them the adequate time that vital sign needs to stay balanced.

This is where the word *balance* comes into life. Balance, in our world, has *nothing* to do with fairness or comparison between the four. Balance is strict with your level of being at peace with that area of your life. Not that you are at peace, meaning you are just okay with what is happening there. But you are peaceful in a very strong and active way, meaning that you have given that part of your life the time and effort it needs.

We do our 90 Day Goal Rush, which is our one-on-one coaching program where we guarantee results or offer money back! It is something that most clients ask how we can do it, and it is an easy answer. We know we can show people quickly how to live a fulfilled life if they just give the Four Vital Signs of Fulfillment the time they need. All of a sudden, they are able to increase their overall performance in all areas of their life.

The average person, when we go through the goals they are working toward over the ninety days we work with them, only needs about ten to twelve hours a week. The issue is not that they do not have time. It is that they are living a boring and lifeless life, with no fulfillment and no real reason besides to survive for the next day. **Using Reverse Planning gives you the ability to schedule your time you need to live the life you need before someone else steals that time from you that you can never get back.**

A simple solution is to take the 168 hours a week and find ten hours of that is about 5 percent of the week to live the life you want to live—get after it! You can live an intentional and fulfilling life!

THE VALUE OF THE SYSTEM

We have used this system that we call the LP for years and have introduced it to individuals all over the world. Because of this, I want to introduce it, but there is no need to reinvent the wheel. We released a number-one international bestseller titled **Motivate the Unmotivated: A Proven System for Sustainable Motivation**, in which we explain how to use our LP to help motivate yourself and others. This chapter is right out of the book because it explains the whole system along with the questions to ask yourself when it comes to building your own intentional week.

USING THE LP AS A MOTIVATEE

Get More Done for You

Failing to plan is planning to fail.

The common basis of decision-making, for almost every lifeform on earth, revolves around one central principle: What will help them live longer? Think about trees. You probably learned in school that the way you determine the age of a tree is by counting the number of rings in its trunk. What you might not know is that those rings appear when under an immense amount of stress.

These same forces happen in our lives. A good friend of mine, Dr. Austin Cohen, uses the term "Expansion Cycles." These are times in our life that are hard. We're struggling, we're going through a lot of stress, but it's during these times that we could experience the most growth.

Trees try to grow as high as they can because they know that the higher they get, the more likely they are to receive the sunlight necessary for life. Branches aren't just for decoration. They're intentional offshoots that the plant uses to send leaves to an area where the sun is shining. Growing branches and leaves is stressful for the tree and takes a lot out of it, but these are tangible examples of growth. In the winter, the tree sheds its leaves and rests. The tree faithfully follows these work and rest cycles every year until it dies.

Humans aren't as consistent. When we get out of our rhythm or routine, we become less effective, and our intentional growth slows tremendously. Some people avoid routines on purpose, thinking that it will inhibit their freedom. What they don't realize is that when they refuse to take part in intentionally creating a rhythm, that doesn't mean it doesn't happen. It just gets built without them. We all live in some kind of routine. The difference between successful and unsuccessful people is often the part they play in shaping that.

Having a routine doesn't mean you become a workaholic. Rest is just as important as work, and having the right balance gives you the best chance at growth. Sometimes it's the right call to binge-watch Netflix for eight hours—just make sure it is an intentional call. My father recently retired from a phenomenally successful career as a dentist. He built a substantial practice over several decades, raised four kids, maintained a happy marriage, and was active in the community. This all took a tremendous amount of hard work. He was watching me speak one time, and when the moment for audience participation came, he asked for the mic. I'll admit, I was a little nervous. Even though I speak professionally, having one of my parents in the audience, now with a mic, is far from typical. He turned around, looked at the audience, and said: "I've known about the LP system for a while. I'm retired now, so you might think I'm done with systems. That isn't true. Systems are just as important now as at any point in my life. I have found when you have the freedom to do nothing, it's really easy to just do nothing."

That's a profound statement. Rest has a purpose and is absolutely necessary. When we don't have a system in place, though, rest ceases to be deliberate and becomes our default. Then we stop growing. Living a balanced and enjoyable life involves mimicking nature's growth patterns. We have to stay in a rhythm and use a system that allows us to do this. This is where the LP system comes into play. It was designed with nature in mind and takes only a small investment of twenty minutes at the beginning of the week and five minutes each night to map out the next day.

As you go through the following nine questions, write out your answers. If it is easy for you, or your motivatee, to answer all nine questions quickly and accurately, then you have an amazing and unusual grasp on your life. If it takes you time to really get to the heart of these, like most people, you will be amazed at the results just by answering these questions before you or your motivatees start the week. Maria and I do this every week, then share our answers with each other. I would challenge you to do the same with the ones you are trying to motivate or build a relationship with.

1. **One-Word Focus:** What's the one word you should focus on to accomplish what you need to get done this week?
2. **Quote:** What's a quote that will define what you mean by your one-word focus?
3. **Gratitude:** What are you grateful for?
4. **Weekly Wisdom:** What did you learn last week that you can implement this week?
   a. Message us through our website or social media, and I will personally send you one each week for free.
5. **Pulse Check:** How well have you balanced your time/life in the Four Vital Signs of Fulfillment (Internal/Relational/Physical/Professional)?
6. **Goals:** What do you want to accomplish this week in the Four Vital Signs of Fulfillment?
7. **Brain Dump:** What do you logistically need to do this week?
8. **Event Manager:** What are your top priorities based on your goals and urgency?

9 **Daily Schedule:** What events do you have scheduled or need to schedule?

This is the basic structure for the LP system, and it will allow you to see what you need to accomplish clearly. I use the LP when I'm at work as well as on vacation. Staying within the system allows me to be more productive when I'm working and more relaxed when I'm not. Most people live like they're trying to put together the puzzle of life without even taking it out of the box. That invites a lot of frustration. The best way to solve a puzzle is to dump it out on a large area where you can see the big picture, then search for the outside pieces so you can build a framework. Once this is complete, finishing the puzzle becomes simple and rewarding.

That's what the LP system does. It allows you and your motivatee to brain dump and get everything out where you can see it. Then you can create a structure that puts everything else in your life in the proper place. Once that's done, going through the motions, just like finishing a puzzle, becomes a simple task.

Try this for the next four weeks. Make sure you, as a motivator, do this. Take the time to understand the LP system. You can do it with your motivatee at the same time if you want, but the key here is for you to use it yourself. If you want, we have physical LPs that you can order from our website to help guide you and your motivatee through the process. But using those nine questions every week will add to the structure of your life significantly, even without the physical LP.

If you want to go deeper into this powerful system, I encourage you to get a copy of *Motivate the Unmotivated: A Proven System for Sustainable Motivation* (available on Amazon).

THE VALUE OF THE PROCESS

I believe focusing on the process is the most underutilized technique to achieve goals. The process in the past has been taught like this.

- Set a goal.
- Focus on the goal.
- Achieve the goal.

This works, but if you have ever experienced the feeling of setting the goal and achieving the goal, there are many more steps than just Set, Focus, Achieve. For example, there are highs, lows, and plateaus when going from Setting a goal to Achieving a goal. There are steps forward, backward, and any direction necessary when going from setting a goal to achieving a goal. The reason most people do not experience the process of setting and achieving goals is that they are focusing on those two parts. Setting the goal takes very little time. The moment you achieve the goal is exactly that. A moment, an instant, almost such a short time that it is hard to measure it.

So when we say "focus on the goal," what does that mean? We know where we want to go; once we see that and know where we want to go, we then need to act as if we are driving a car in that direction. We are aware of the direction we are going, but I need to focus on the ride, which we see as the process of achieving the goal. If we were driving across the country from New York to California, we would be foolish to look for California signs. In fact, you would never get out of New York if you were focusing on achieving the goal the whole time. You need to pay attention to street names, other vehicles, exits on and onto highways, gas levels of the car, bathroom needs of the people you are driving with, hotels you are staying, and restaurants you will be eating in.

The act of Setting (I am going to California) and achieving (I'm here) is simple but will not get you where you want to go. Instead, we need to focus on the process. That is what brings value to setting and achieving the goal as the work you need to put into it, which is what makes it "worth it" in the end.

We work with employees at Twitter, and one of the best comments we received from an individual on Twitter was, "This system brings value to the process." **Most people spend their whole time looking at what they are going after that they miss out on what they are experiencing right now.** We focus on the end goal, but we make sure, using our LP Structure of Success, that the weekly planning and our daily actions are set so that when we do them enough times, it will lead us to where we are going.

Here is how we instruct our clients to get started, and as you have heard throughout the book, repetition is key—excerpt from the previous chapter, The Value of the Experience.

We will break down some of our most effective principles we have successfully discovered through working with clients all over the world. I would ask that you take the *truly* short time it takes and read the intro chapters and the breakdown of what we will be doing each week. You do not need to go into what we want you to read about each day, but if you are an overachiever, go for the whole book, from front to back. This way, you fully understand what we are doing, where we are going, and how we are getting there.

Once you have gotten these principles understood, we can get started on the work. If for some reason, you just want to get into the work, the system will work for you but will be a bit more challenging for you to keep focused and disciplined, but hey, this is your week. You got this book because you want it to be intentional. Your choices are what will or will not make this work, as it has for many in the past.

So we have set up a four-week process that will fill each month. Because of how we know repetition is key and learning while doing is helpful, you will be going through the same four weeks, three separate times. However, I ask each week, once you feel you have mastered the first step, you can go to the next. Some people spend all ninety days just on the first step, and others seem to get all three in the ninety days. So for the first cycle, through it, you will be in the mindset of the Mentee, then as a Peer to me, and finally as a Mentor to me. That is right; you will go through this as the student who will quickly become the teacher. As you go through the program, depending on which cycle you are in, this is where your mindset should be:

- **Mentee:** This is when I am telling you what to do and why to do it, and you are to do it how I teach it.
- **Peer:** This is when I am telling you what to do and why to do it, and you are to do it how *you* feel it needs to be done in your life.
- **Mentor:** This is when I am telling you what to do and why to do it, and you are to do it so you can teach someone else how to do it.

If it sounds strange that you will be repeating the same things multiple times, it can only mean that you haven't experienced how simple life can be lived when proper systems are implemented. We are all creatures of habit. You have routines that, when you do not do, make you feel "off." Everything we do and teach is to make creating these routines simple, easy, and, most importantly, effective.

Life is not supposed to be hard. Books like these are not supposed to be confusing. Simplicity is the key, and systems are what make simplicity also effective. We have been told our whole lives we need to work hard, and if we don't feel it, then it is not working. It takes implementing proper systems in your life that consistently are implemented and gaining a compound effect on the actions you previously took. It is not about working hard; it is about finding systems that help life be more fulfilled and each week be more intentional.

Remember, this is not a race to the finish line but a chance for you to stride with confidence through an intentional and fulfilled life! Remember, you will not change your life in a week, but if you change the weeks in your life, no matter where you are, you can get where you want to be.

In the chapter before this, I explained the nine questions we use to create our intentional week. In the second chapter of this book, I explained how this program would work so that this system will become a simple routine in your life. It will feel strange at first, but once you make it through this program once, it will become your new normal. **The key is to remember that systems bring freedom, and rhythm brings peace.** The system was taught to you throughout the book, and especially in the previous chapter. But rhythm takes action and experience. This is the next step in creating your Intentional Week.

3 CYCLES OF ACHIEVING THE INTENTIONAL WEEK

Everything we teach or coach on at Life Pulse is based on ninety-day cycles. Ninety days/three months/one quarter has been shown to us as the best way to set goals, follow through with goals, and achieve goals. Also, the key to successfully implementing something is through repetition. The final key to allow a system to stick as part of your life is simultaneously learning and doing at the same time. We want to give you a solution for all three in this program.

We will breakdown some of our most effective principles we have discovered through working successfully with clients all over the world. I would ask that you take the very short time it takes and read the intro chapters and the breakdown of what we will be doing each week. You do not need to go into what we want you to read about each day, but if you are an overachiever, go for the whole book, from front to back. This way, you fully understand what we are doing, where we are going, and how we are getting there.

Once you have gotten these principles understood, we can get started on the work. If for some reason, you just want to get into the work, the system will work for you, but it will be a bit more challenging for you to keep focused and disciplined, but hey, this is your week. You got this book because you want it to be intentional. Your choices are what will or will not make this work, as it has for many in the past.

We have set up a four-week process, which will be cycled each month. Because of how we know repetition is key and learning while doing is helpful, you will be going through the four-week cycle three separate times. However, I ask each week, once you feel you have mastered the first step, you can go to the next. Some people spend all ninety days just on the first step, and others seem to get all three in the ninety days. For the first cycle, you will be in the mindset of the Mentee to me, then as a Peer to me, and finally as a Mentor to me. That is right; you will go through this as the student who will quickly become the teacher. As you go through the program, depending on which cycle you are in, this is where your mindset should be:

- **Mentee**: This is when I am telling you what to do and why to do it, and you are to do it how I teach it.
- **Peer**: This is when I am telling you what to do and why to do it, and you are to do it how you feel it needs to be done in your life.
- **Mentor**: This is when I am telling you what to do and why to do it, and you are to do it so you can teach someone else how to do it.

If it sounds strange that you will be repeating the same things multiple times, it can only mean that you haven't experienced how simple life can be lived when proper systems are implemented. We are all creatures of habit. You have routines that, when you do not do, make you feel "off." Everything we do and teach is to make creating these routines simple, easy, and most importantly, effective.

Life is not supposed to be hard. Books like these are not supposed to be confusing. Simplicity is the key, and systems are what makes simplicity also effective. We have been told our whole life we need to work hard, and if we don't feel it, then it is not working. A mentor once told me that making money is fun but making a lot of money—well, that becomes boring. When I was young and first starting out, I could not wrap my head around it. I feel making money would be fun, but why would it be boring to make a lot of money? The reason is to make a couple hundred thousand a year is challenging, but in order to make more than that consistently, it takes implementing proper systems in your life that consistently are implemented and gaining a compound effect on the actions you previously took. It is not about working hard; it is about finding systems that help life be more fulfilled and each week be more intentional.

Remember, this is not a race to the finish line but a chance for you to stride with confidence through an intentional and fulfilled life! Remember, you will not change your life in a week, but if you change the weeks in your life, no matter where you are, you can get where you want to be.

Cycle 1: Mentee

Mindset: This is when I am telling you what to do and why to do it, and you are to do it how I teach it.

As stated before, the process is very undervalued in today's society because we are searching for immediate gratification. The only way we find to go from not knowing to knowing is memorization. This is how most people make it through school, but this is not learning. There are some benefits to memorization, such as being able to recall information quickly. For certain parts of life, that is *extremely* valuable and a skill set we should all work on.

But that is when you jump from not knowing to knowing. But I want this to be sustainable. This is like not knowing someone's name to knowing someone's name. That is basically an instant. But what happens the second that person walks away for most of us? Their name is completely forgotten. But if as we get to know people, even if, in that first introduction, we have a powerful conversation that lets me learn a bit more about the person, the likelihood of me knowing not only their name but also a bit more of who they are is much higher.

In our philosophy, we have two steps before we worry about before fully understanding, as we feel some action is required to get a full understanding of what we do. This week, what I want you to do is just learn the topics we are teaching and implement them yourself.

Although we are taught to question everything, which I feel is valuable, before we do that, try your best to prove them right. The worst that can happen when it comes to the information we are offering is that you know for sure it is not for you or if you *really* put the effort to overcome any bad habits and lack of discipline you might have faced in the past, and you will see how it can actually help your week.

Take the following subjects, and I want you to spend twenty minutes that day understanding them and then implementing them. The read will be no more than ten minutes, and then you will have the other ten minutes to make sure you are using the tool for that day or the next day. As you work through the weeks, make sure you do not forget what you learned the days before.

No matter when you decide to start, think of how *you* can use this for *your* life. In life, truth is constant, but application changes. You can apply this as you see fit.

Cycle 2: Peer

Mindset: I tell you what to do and why to do it. You do it how *you* feel it needs to be done in your life.

Congratulations on getting through the first four weeks of this program. As you can see, I am not looking for you to take a lot of big steps. Instead, I want you to get used to taking multiple little steps that will build into big results.

You made it through the first cycle with the mindset of learning, but now, I want you to go through it as if you and I are in this together. I mean this as you now know the system, you have done the system, so because of that, you should be able to make it more of your own.

When you come back through something you were told to do the last cycle, think through how well you implemented it. If it was not as well as you feel it could have been, here is a second chance to be able to do it better. Sometimes, when you are first introduced to something, it takes a lot of energy to understand, and implementation is delayed due to our focus on understanding. Well, now you are relearning some.

For those who you feel you have implemented well, think of what you can do to make it better. Could you have done it in a different way? Could you have focused differently? Could you have taken different actions?

Now is the time to be able to work on this as if we are a partner in this. Think about it as if I am a friend of yours who is going through this with you. (You also can invite any friend to be a part of it.)

Think through this, as you are not new at this anymore. You have the experience, and you understand "what you should be doing." Now is the time to see the full potential of this.

The rest of the book will be the next cycle in our program. Keep moving your bookmark to the next page. Keep seeing the progress. You have already read most of them, so for some of the longer writeups, we have shortened them to keep it one page per task of the day.

I am excited to go through Cycle 2 with you as a peer now that you understand what we do.

Let's get started!

Cycle 3: Mentor

Mindset: I tell you what to do and why to do it. You do it while you think of how you can teach someone else how to do it.

This is when the student becomes the teacher. I mean that literally. You have gone through the program twice, and you are now going onto the third cycle. This is the cycle you can repeat for the rest of your life if you'd like, and I want you to keep this mindset as we discussed in a mode where you take what we teach, and you make it perfect for you.

You are the one who needs to use this system for the rest of your weeks. So, you have done it twice; now, make it your own.

Remember that truth is consistent, and application can change. So let's adapt this, so it best fits what you need.

Go through all four weeks of this last cycle and change what you need from an application perspective to be yours.

The most successful individuals take systems and make them their own. As you go through the next four weeks, think of this as a mentor or a teacher. How would you teach this to someone else? How would you implement this for the team you work with? How would you make this system yours?

Now that you are the teacher, it is time for you to get started. Like in the second cycle, we will write summaries of the Task of the Day for you to focus on and any necessary notes for you to go through. Keep moving the book market, keep taking notes, and keep progressing.

Keep us posted, and enjoy becoming a master in intentionality. Enjoy the benefits of what you are going to experience as you make this system yours and teach others how they can live an intentional life.

You are four weeks away from completing the cycle.

Cycle 1 Mindset: Mentee	Cycle 2 Mindset: Peer	Cycle 3 Mindset: Mentor
You are to do it as close as you can based on how I teach it.	*You do it how you feel it needs to be done in your life.*	*You think of how you can teach someone else how to do it.*

WEEK 1

Learn: *Receive the knowledge with implementation in mind.*

In *Motivate the Unmotivated*, I discuss an argument that we all have had at some point in my life. Who is responsible for learning: the teacher or the student? We made the argument that it is the teacher's job to teach (present the information); however, it is the student's job to learn (bring value to the information presented). We have found that the best way to make sure we, as students, get the most out of the information we are exposed to is to learn with implementation in mind.

How are you going to be able to use whatever information you are experiencing? That is right. Get selfish on this portion. Take the information you are getting and think through how you are going to be able to use it in your life. When you do this, it will be easier to comprehend, and you will experience your desired results much faster.

Remember your focus as you go through these next seven days is to learn with implementation in mind. You can start on whatever day you want. Traditionally, it would be that Monday starts the week, so we will start PTT (Planning Tomorrow Today) on Sunday or day one. What we have found works best is to jump on the pre-existing cycle you have for weeks. If your week starts on Wednesdays, then you can start your day one on Tuesday or Sunday. It really does not matter, as long as you have the seven-day cycle.

☐ Cycle 1 Mindset: <u>Mentee</u>	☐ Cycle 2 Mindset: <u>Peer</u>	☐ Cycle 3 Mindset: <u>Mentor</u>
You are to do it as close as you can based on how I teach it.	*You do it how you feel it needs to be done in your life.*	*You think of how you can teach someone else how to do it.*

Plan Your First Week
Week 1, Day 1 *(Traditionally Sunday)*

TASK OF THE DAY (TOD)

Once you have reviewed the LP system, you can use your LP or just use the nine questions to help you get your week set up. Set aside a select amount of time to plan out your week. When you understand the LP system, it usually can be done in twenty minutes or less. Personally, we like to take our time with it. Maria and I, before we share our plan with each other, we do our own plan for the week. It is relaxing to take our time and think through what is happening for the week.

At first, it may be stressful because you see *all* you have to do for the first time on paper, but after a few weeks of doing this (usually two to four), you see that you will be able to handle whatever comes your way because you have a system to lean on. The mental relief of knowing you can deal with whatever life throws your way is worth this step.

Intentional Tips:
* Check the mindset box when you have completed this day's cycle.
* To dive deeper, refer to chapter "The Value of the System.".

Heavy Load Monday And Get As Much Done As You Can

Week 1, Day 2 *(Traditionally Monday)*

TASK OF THE DAY (TOD)

Some people like to slowly get into the week, and if that is you, it is fine to do it that way. What we have found works wonders is heavy load the front end of the week. With how fast life throws us off our desired path, the concept of "I will get to that" is filled with good intentions but tends to not happen.

Think of the last time you left for vacation. When people leave for vacation, it is like they turn a level of productivity that they have never shown before. If they start work on Monday and are leaving on Thursday for a long weekend, they are somehow able to do an *entire* week of work in just the first three days. I believe this is because they do not have time to get distracted.

This is how we need to think of our first two to three days in the week. We start with day one and load it up so we can get as much done right away. As the week gets started, we get pulled by new tasks thrown our way or people asking for new things to be done.

So the way we resolve this is the same mentality of "I don't have time to get distracted."

Don't make it impossible to complete, but make sure you load your tasks on Monday and the front end of your week so that you can relax at the end of the week. Do this, and you will see quickly that you do not need a full week to do the things you do weekly. You have *a lot* more time than you expect.

Plan Tomorrow Today (PTT)
Week 1, Day 3 *(Traditionally Tuesday)*

TASK OF THE DAY (TOD)

Make sure you are taking time each night to plan tomorrow, today! Give yourself five to ten minutes at the end of the night or at the end of the business day, and plan the next day. I like to end my night this way because it will give me calmness and confidence in what is coming tomorrow, and I have it under control as much as I can.

This is a simple task, and I have found doing this allows me to sleep soundly through the night, and even better is I tend to wake up with the answer on how to get started. It is like as I am sleeping, my brain is starting to figure out some of the problems I am looking to take on the next day.

For this task, just take the time at night or the end of your day and list out the tasks that have to get done. If it feels overwhelming, do not worry. By using the tools like the Event Manager, Survival Shapes, and Intentional Procrastination (which we will get to later), you will be able to manage any size list and any size task.

Make the list tonight, enjoy the good night's sleep, and let's get it taken care of tomorrow.

Intentional Tips:
- Check the mindset box when you have completed this day's cycle.
- To dive deeper, refer to chapter "The Value of the Planning."

Survival Shapes
Week 1, Day 4 *(Traditionally Wednesday)*

TASK OF THE DAY (TOD)

If you are following our daily steps, at this point, you have planned your week on Day 1, made sure you heavy-loaded the front of your week with tasks, and took advantage of the time by using our PTT techniques. So even with all of that, there is the question: where do I start?

Now, let's see how we are going to survive this day. I say "survive" because sometimes that is what days feel like. Also, I say "survive" because when we survive, it is an assumption that we are doing whatever it takes to survive. That means we are willing to take chances, try to figure things out, but most importantly, we are going to need to conserve energy.

Clients waste too much energy on trying too hard, dealing with unneeded stress, and worrying about things that have nothing to do with the task at hand. All of this *drains* our energy. Our brain cannot multitask as much as we try to act as it can. When we hear people say they can multitask, we will ask them to change the name to "partial task" because that is all they can do at best.

So let's take that list and remember that the goal is not to get *everything* done but it is to get the *right things* done. So, we will get three Survival Shapes. Now, you can use this technique if you have a list that is just too long, but we need to breakdown our events into three categories.

<u>**Circle:**</u> No matter what (NMW), the task has to happen that day
<u>**Square:**</u> It doesn't have to happen, but we really should get it done

Triangle: Tasks that would be nice to get done as time permits (ATP)

If you are like most clients of ours, you may say that everything on your list for the day has to get done. Otherwise, why would it be on your list? This thought comes from how you have been trying to process your thoughts in your head. When we have it out on paper as you've done, keep reminding yourself, the goal is not to get everything done but to get the right things done.

So to stop you from being like the high-school kid who is studying and highlights the whole textbook because *it all* could be on the test, let's look at this with some more logic and less emotion.

The average person can effectively do seven meaningful tasks in a day. These are not routine tasks but things that will take some dedicated brainpower. So let's work with seven. When you look at the list you created during your PTT session, do the following in order priority.

ORDER OF PRIORITIES

---

1. **Circle the one task**, yes, only one, that you are going to do no matter what (NMW).

2. **Square the next three tasks** that you feel you need to get done (GID).

3. **Triangle the next three tasks** that you feel you would like to get done as time permits (ATP).

Then, get comfortable. This means that your day *could* be done if you want. This is how we ensure the ability to disconnect and enjoy life. This is also how we manage crisis mode. There are some things that, no matter what (NMW) happens, need to get done. There are other things that we need to get done (GID) but could wait if there was a good enough reason, and then there are other tasks that we should do as time permits (ATP).

Life happens, and when it does, we do need to be able to be reactive. The best way to be reactive is to be proactive before it occurs. This is why we make the commitment to these seven tasks the night before, so when we start the day, we get started on the right task in the right direction.

Intentional Tips:
- Check the mindset box when you have completed this day's cycle.
- To dive deeper, refer to chapter "The Value of the Planning."

Time Chunks

Week 1, Day 5 *(Traditionally Thursday)*

TASK OF THE DAY (TOD)

We have found that there are three types of goals. The first two you may have been introduced to, which we call action-based and result-based goals. We have found that there is an even better way to achieve long-term sustainable growth. I believe that is called time-based goals.

I learned about this when training for my first Ironman race. My coach would never give me a distance to go. He would always give me an amount of time to go on a ride. It would drive me nuts, but it opened my eyes to a more effective way to achieve any goal I want. I started calling these goals Time Chunks and Time Buckets.

I want you to pick a big goal you are trying to achieve. Even if it is a task that needs to be done, but you just do not want to do it (i.e., employee reviews, expense reports, cleaning the garage, organizing desk, etc.). It doesn't matter what the task is; just choose it and follow these simple instructions.

Pick a time frame you would like to work. It can be any time frame *below* ninety minutes. We have some people who use thirty, sixty, or ninety-minute Time Chunks. We have other clients who use the pomodoro technique, which suggests you use twenty-five-minute Time Chunks. Again, it can be *anything* below ninety minutes, and find what works best for you.

Now set a Time Chunk. Set a specific amount of time (Time Chunk) for you to work on the task at hand. You do not need to finish it. You just need to dedicate that time to the task we are talking about.

You will quickly find that you are able to get any task done, no matter how big or small, if you dedicate enough Time Chunks to that task.

This seems like common sense, but it is not commonly used—a simple solution for the seemingly chronic issue.

Try it today and use it as much as you can for whatever tasks you may need to complete.

Intentional Tips:
- Check the mindset box when you have completed this day's cycle.
- To dive deeper, refer to chapter "The Value of the Week."

□ Cycle 1 Mindset: <u>Mentee</u>	□ Cycle 2 Mindset: <u>Peer</u>	□ Cycle 3 Mindset: <u>Mentor</u>
You are to do it as close as you can based on how I teach it.	*You do it how you feel it needs to be done in your life.*	*You think of how you can teach someone else how to do it.*

Catch Up: Pushing Things Off To Next Week
Week 1, Day 6 *(Traditionally Friday)*

TASK OF THE DAY (TOD)

Respect your time. Make sure you are comfortable knowing, "I will get to that next week." We sit in our week and feel like we have too much to do. At that same moment, we are quick to offer our time up to more tasks or more people. Be okay with saying no to things that do not need to happen this week. There is *always* time next week, but there is not always time this week.

Being on day six, you have one day left. Make sure you are not giving more time than you have to others and watch when you act as if it can happen next week.

Also, think about when you need to follow up with someone, do not rush a meeting this week knowing we are going into the weekend. When someone has time, they have excuses. We want people to be able to act quickly after we talk. So if we are coming up on the end of the week, we want to be comfortable, if it is possible, to push things to next week.

The key is to organize the front of your week, so you are heavy-loaded and make sure you are using the back end of your week to get done what is needed. Remember, no one wants to "get started" or make a decision right before the end of the week. Make sure you use your days in a way that allows each day to get maximum effectiveness. .

Intentional Tips:
- Check the mindset box when you have completed this day's cycle.
- To dive deeper, refer to chapter "The Value of the Structure."

☐ Cycle 1 Mindset: <u>Mentee</u>	☐ Cycle 2 Mindset: <u>Peer</u>	☐ Cycle 3 Mindset: <u>Mentor</u>
You are to do it as close as you can based on how I teach it.	*You do it how you feel it needs to be done in your life.*	*You think of how you can teach someone else how to do it.*

No Time Limits: Choose Not To Be Rushed
Week 1, Day 7 *(Traditionally Saturday)*

Task of the Day (TOD)

I am sure you know this but may have never told yourself this, but this is your life, and you are the one who sets the boundaries around how your time is spent. What this means is that you do not need to be as rushed as you may feel that you are. Also, the feeling of "rushed" comes from no external factors. It is just the way you are internalizing what is happening around you. You are not rushed, and you always have the option to slow down.

So here is what I want you to do on this seventh day of the week.

Rest.

There is nothing that *needs* to be done today that you cannot do tomorrow or later in the week. This will be a difficult thing for many people to do, but just let this be your free day of more "being" and less "doing."

Please take care of any responsibilities, but make sure when this day is done, you are fulfilled. This does not mean that you won't be tired from a busy day of being with the family, enjoying activities you like, or anything you decide to do with this day, but this is a day where you need to not allow yourself to be rushed.

We are going to get where we need to go, and we are going to get there on time, but we are not going to turn the house into a military drill to make sure everything is in order before we get out the door.

This is a day that we get to just go with the flow.

For some of you, this will be a relief. For others, the thought of this is making you uncomfortable, but for all of you, when you complete the rest of the program, you will be masters at making the most out of this ability to not be rushed.

Intentional Tips:
- Check the mindset box when you have completed this day's cycle.
- To dive deeper, refer to chapter "The Value of the Structure."

78

WEEK 2

Live: *Experience what you have learned.*

Yeah, we want you to experience before we want you to fully understand what it is we are doing. Please understand, this does not mean that you should blindly follow anything anyone says, but if it does no harm to you, there is power in adding experience into the learning process. There are teaching philosophies from adults to children who focus on this concept specifically, and as we discussed, these things are not things I want you to memorize but instead experience.

In your life, assuming what you are learning is not going to harm you, there is a benefit of doing it before you understand why you should do it. We need to understand what needs to be done and make sure what we are doing is not to the detriment of who we are. This is something that slows down nearly *all* of our clients when they first start working with us. They seem to have issues getting *anything* of substance done because they feel they need to fully understand why it is beneficial, or they confuse the "what." Again, understanding what is being asked to do is totally fine and good to have, so we do it properly. But we do not need to know what will happen by doing it. Outcomes may vary in all situations, and with each client we work with, we see different levels of results. Because of that, as we learn, we learn what we need to do, and we then want to take some action using what we learned, which will help us lead to the true understanding of the value of the task.

Let's jump into Week 2.

☐ Cycle 1 Mindset: <u>Mentee</u> *You are to do it as close as you can based on how I teach it.*	☐ Cycle 2 Mindset: <u>Peer</u> *You do it how you feel it needs to be done in your life.*	☐ Cycle 3 Mindset: <u>Mentor</u> *You think of how you can teach someone else how to do it.*

Discussing Your Plan With Others
Week 2, Day 1 *(Traditionally Sunday)*

TASK OF THE DAY (TOD)

If you live with a spouse or a roommate, we always suggest doing this together. If you do not want to do it with them or you do not have that option, then find a friend to do this with that you would like to support you and whom you would like to support.

The structure is simple. We use the LP Planner, so it gives a clear way to structure intention, but whatever plan you are using, here is what you do.

No matter if it is you and another person or you and a group, you need to do your plan first individually. Using reverse planning, list what you want to do, then what you need to do, and then just do what is important. Once your plan is written out, come together with the other person or group and go through the plan from top to bottom.

Share yours and then hear theirs. It is amazing how disconnected we are from people that we think we are in sync with. We think we know what they want to do, and we think they know what we want to do. When you do this, you will be surprised at how much you know about the other person at times and how far off your assumptions are at other times.

Enjoy this, open a bottle of wine, and let your weekly planning session be more of a celebration than a chore.

Intentional Tips:
• Check the mindset box when you have completed this day's cycle.
• To dive deeper, refer to chapter "The Value of the Planning."

Time Buckets
Week 2, Day 2 *(Traditionally Monday)*

TASK OF THE DAY (TOD)

The goal of today is to find a place to put your tasks as they arrive! This may sound strange, but here is how I can best explain Time Chunks.

I am assuming you have done the dishes in your home before. When you first move into a home, you need to figure out where everything goes, and the kitchen tends to take us the longest. What goes where and whose logic (mine or Maria's) will win for where the oven mitts or the spatulas go. But here is what happens. Once you set it the first time, unless you redo the whole thing, everything has its place.

When you do the dishes and are putting the dishes away, everything has a place, and it makes the process easier to complete and easier to use the item when you need it next time.

For this task, I want you to take some time, review your weeks, and try to categorize some of the repeated things you do. For example, for the businesses I run, I have Time Buckets I save for the day because, as a business owner, I need to do two things: Business Maintenance and Business Growth. I use these buckets so I know where to schedule something in my day. If I have a client who wants to do a coaching call or our tech team needs assistance on something, that will go in the Business Maintenance Bucket. If a new client wants to talk about bringing us onto their team for coaching, that would be scheduled in my Business Growth Time Bucket. Once my time bucket is full, I may not have time that day or that week to do the task, and I know where I need to schedule it later.

Reflect on your day. What are some of the categories of things you need to do each week? Set the appropriate amount of Time Buckets so when someone asked to do something with you or for you to do something for them, you have a Time Bucket where you can put that task, or you can recognize you have done a lot in that area and need to push this task off to the following week.

We use Time Buckets for people in administrative or supportive positions. These people have a big heart and a big appetite to help people. But that big appetite is sometimes like the thirteen-year-old at an all-you-can-eat buffet for the first time. They fill their plate with the intention of finishing everything, but it is just too much for them to finish. In some of our supportive positions that we coach, we have Time Buckets that they can designate to help others. Once those Time Buckets are full, they need to say no or schedule it on their next available Time Bucket.

Build your Time Buckets into your calendar, and you will be amazed how easy it is to fill them and how much more control you will gain over your schedule versus letting others and life dictate what you do and when you do it.

Intentional Tips:
- Check the mindset box when you have completed this day's cycle.
- To dive deeper, refer to chapter "The Value of the Planning."

☐ Cycle 1 Mindset: <u>Mentee</u>	☐ Cycle 2 Mindset: <u>Peer</u>	☐ Cycle 3 Mindset: <u>Mentor</u>
You are to do it as close as you can based on how I teach it.	*You do it how you feel it needs to be done in your life.*	*You think of how you can teach someone else how to do it.*

Keep Meetings With Yourself As You Would Others

Week 2, Day 3 *(Traditionally Tuesday)*

Task of the Day (TOD)

It is okay to give time to yourself. In fact, when you think about why you are doing what you are doing, it is so you can live the life you want. Even if you are in a survival mode currently, it is to live the life you want. I can tell you from working with individuals all over the world that you can live the life you want now if you just add a bit of intention to it and keep the meetings with yourself.

Most people are quick at giving up their time to others. I am talking about moving mountains to get to a meeting with someone else, even changing your day because a coworker asks if you want to get lunch together. As you know, the philosophies we believe and teach, interacting and being with others is extremely important, but even more important is that you keep meetings you set with yourself.

Today, you need to keep your meetings with yourself and schedule out the other meetings you may need to have with yourself. Some of the things we need to do during these meetings are focus on our internal, relational, physical, vital signs. Have a meeting to read the book you've wanted to read; have a meeting to get to the gym a couple of times this week. Have a meeting to sit with your kids and play with toys. Have a meeting to have a conversation with your significant other. Have a meeting with yourself, resting.

I mean it! Schedule time for yourself, and when someone asks if they can meet you at that time, try to offer another option. It doesn't matter if it is not as important according to what the world considers important. The level of importance is subjective and only has as much value that you see in each task.

Here is extra credit: If you ever think, say, or complain about not having enough "time for you" and you are not intentionally scheduling these things, stop that now. Take action versus complain, and you actually get a result worth giving energy to.

Intentional Tips:
- Check the mindset box when you have completed this day's cycle.
- To dive deeper, refer to chapter "The Value of the Structure."

☐ Cycle 1 Mindset: <u>Mentee</u> *You are to do it as close as you* *can based on how I teach it.*	☐ Cycle 2 Mindset: <u>Peer</u> *You do it how you feel it needs* *to be done in your life.*	☐ Cycle 3 Mindset: <u>Mentor</u> *You think of how you can teach* *someone else how to do it.*

Plan Versus Execution
Week 2, Day 4 *(Traditionally Wednesday)*

TASK OF THE DAY (TOD)

Stick to the plan. At this point, you are planning at the beginning of the week, and then you are also planning the night before for the next day (PTT), so I want to challenge you today to *just* follow your plan. If anything else comes up, push it to tomorrow unless it is a life-or-death issue.

There is a freeing feeling when you recognize that you can keep the plan that you set as long as you make that choice at the begging of the day. Today, we are going to execute our plan. We are not going to change our plan or alter our plan. We are going to just execute.

Be okay if your day is ending earlier than normal; there is a lot you can do when all you focus on is execution. Enjoy this day, as this will help free your mind for many of the days, weeks, and months to come.

Intentional Tips:
- Check the mindset box when you have completed this day's cycle.
- To dive deeper, refer to chapter "The Value of the Experience"

Stop Wasting Time On Others
Week 2, Day 5 *(Traditionally Thursday)*

TASK OF THE DAY (TOD)

Today, you are going to take back the influence others may have on you. Stop wasting your time on them. We spend a lot of time looking at what others are doing, so I am going to ask you for today to focus on keeping yourself from focusing on other people's lives, actions, comments, etc.

Today, live your life. Today, focus on you. Disregard the distractions that we allow others to be for us. This does not mean disregarding others. This is just a simple way for you to realize how much time we waste on other people through social media and let others impact our day and mindset.

Enjoy this day of release from the continuous pressure we feel from seeing others' lives every day. Live your life. Be intentional to only let what is happening in your world affect you today. If you'd like, you can go back to worrying about things out of your control tomorrow, but I feel when you experience a day where you intentionally ignore the distractions, you will avoid them even more than before.

Intentional Tips:
* Check the mindset box when you have completed this day's cycle.
* To dive deeper, refer to chapter "The Value of the Week."

Structure Brings Freedom, And Rhythm Brings Peace

Week 2, Day 6 *(Traditionally Friday)*

TASK OF THE DAY (TOD)

In 2020, the world was struck with a pandemic unlike anything history has ever seen. The virus itself was an issue, but the impact it had on the entire world (even those not infected) was unlike anything seen before.

In this time of uncertainty, we were watching clients fall apart, but when we really broke it down, we saw that for those who were not infected with the virus or dealing with loved ones who were, two things were taken from us: our structure and rhythm of our life. It turns out, in most negative situations, the situation has to be dealt with, but the impact on our life does not need to be globally affected.

Meaning, if we are having an issue at work, it does not need to affect all areas of our lives. During this pandemic, we started sharing this philosophy with our clients, and we want you to take this statement and make sure you are focusing on it today.

Structure Brings Freedom and Rhythm Brings Peace

When we are dealing with issues in our lives, this is how isolated issues creep into other areas they do not need to. We are out of rhythm, or we have little structure in our lives.

So here is what you get to do today: check your structure. If you are using the LP, this is the structure we have found works best for most, but whatever structure you have in your life, intentionally recognize it and make any needed tweaks to make it part of your days and weeks.

Then, let's get back into rhythm. It is like tuning an instrument. We do not always need to make drastic adjustments. Sometimes, it is just a small tweak. For most, it is just being intentional about recognizing the rhythm of your life.

Take five minutes to write out the structure of your life. Then, take another five minutes and write out the rhythm that allows you to operate best. Write these down and live by them today!

Intentional Tips:
- Check the mindset box when you have completed this day's cycle.
- To dive deeper, refer to chapter "The Value of the Week."

No Fear! Choose Not To Act Out Of Fear Today
Week 2, Day 7 *(Traditionally Saturday)*

TASK OF THE DAY (TOD)

You made it another week. *Great* job. Today is the second intentional day of rest, and after the last week, it is much needed. We are going to make a choice today that seems like common sense, but as we have talked about in this book, just because it is common sense does not mean it is commonly done.

Today, it is your job to choose not to act out of fear. Fear is a debilitating controller of us when we allow it to affect our actions. Understand fear is healthy and will save us from a lot of harmful experiences but only when it is used for what it should be. It is used as a warning, something we should not ignore but should not bow down to. Address it, bring it into the decision-making process, along with all other outcomes, and then make a decision.

Fear as your master will destroy your life. Fear as your master, when you are unaware of it, will destroy your life and those around you. Put fear in its place on this day of rest and review your actions through the last week. How many did you let fear push you in a direction that you see now as incorrect? As you review what you experienced the past week, think about how you are going to overcome it next week.

For today, enjoy a day where fear has no place in your life. It can come in as a thought, but it does not have control over you today as it may have had yesterday. Fear is a powerful tool when used properly but a dangerous weapon when used against ourselves.

Intentional Tips:
*   Check the mindset box when you have completed this day's cycle.
*   To dive deeper, refer to chapter "The Value of the Planning."

WEEK 3

Understand: tying learning to living to gain a concrete understanding

We are now trying to understand what we need for this process. Now that you went from Learn and Live, we can now start to Understand. This seems like the opposite of what we normally would do. We wait to understand to assume we can learn or live.

So, as you go through this week, focus on the understanding of what we are doing.

You will notice that the tasks of each day for the next seven days are going to give you a better understanding of why we are doing what we are doing. You get to experience this next week to really engrave this in your daily actions.

LP Structure Of Success
Week 3, Day 1 *(Traditionally Sunday)*

TASK OF THE DAY (TOD)

We know that our structure of success works in any part of our life. So today, we are going to make sure that you have an action you take in each of the stages. Here is a list of the tools we have seen work best. Review them and confirm that these work for you, or if you need to do something differently, fill it in on the chart below.

LP Structure of Success	Suggested Tool (all can be found at www.LifePulseInc.com)
Daily Action	i90 Challenge
Weekly Planning	LP Planner
Monthly Celebration	Life Date
Quarterly Review	¼ Life Review
Annual Retreat	5R Retreat (Review, Rest, Refine, Relax, Refocus)

Do one of the following actions:

Get involved in a daily action program like i90 or anything you'd like.

Select a weekly planning system to follow.

Set a date with your significant other or the person closest to you in your life to chat about the good and the bad in life.

Schedule the first day of next quarter to review the previous ninety days.

Select a date this year where you will do your own (or couple or group) annual retreat.

You can do as many of these as you'd like, but I just want you to make sure you do one of these today. They all will help, but we do not need to make huge leaps when we can easily make consistent steps.

☐ Cycle 1 Mindset: <u>Mentee</u> *You are to do it as close as you can based on how I teach it.*	☐ Cycle 2 Mindset: <u>Peer</u> *You do it how you feel it needs to be done in your life.*	☐ Cycle 3 Mindset: <u>Mentor</u> *You think of how you can teach someone else how to do it.*

Four Vital Signs Of Fulfillment

Week 3, Day 2 *(Traditionally Monday)*

Task of the Day (TOD)

Each day, I want to make sure I am giving at least thought to these four vital signs of fulfillment. Not that I need to do a lot of actions toward each, but they should run through my head each day. How am I growing internally, relationally, physically, and professionally today?

I want you to think about what you are doing daily and if you are even involved in these parts of your life. Most will do some, but few will do all. I want you to make sure today you not only think of each of these, but I want you to do something for each of these.

If you are doing the i90 challenge along with this book (which is recommended), then you should be already doing this (or you are losing points). Enjoy today's balance that you will experience and the feeling of fulfillment as the day comes to an end if you take action in each vital sign.

To access the i90 challenge for free, please go to www.LifePulseInc.com/i90.

Intentional Tips:
- Check the mindset box when you have completed this day's cycle.
- To dive deeper, refer to chapter "The Value of the Flow."

☐ Cycle 1 Mindset: <u>Mentee</u> *You are to do it as close as you* *can based on how I teach it.*	☐ Cycle 2 Mindset: <u>Peer</u> *You do it how you feel it needs* *to be done in your life.*	☐ Cycle 3 Mindset: <u>Mentor</u> *You think of how you can teach* *someone else how to do it.*

Pulse Check: The Trajectory Of Life
Week 3, Day 3 *(Traditionally Tuesday)*

TASK OF THE DAY (TOD)

"Check yo self before you wreck yo self!" was a piece of poetry that should live on forever and be a mantra for most of our lives. O'Shea Jackson, a.k.a. Ice Cube, told us this in 1992, and if more people would listen to him, they could live a life with a lot fewer regrets. Not all of what he wrote would apply to everyone, but today, this is what I want you to do: "Check yo self before you wreck yo self."

Take a minute and take inventory of how you are doing in these four vital signs of fulfillment. How did you do last week? How are you doing this week? Take the time to make the small adjustments now, so you do not have big regrets later.

Intentional Tips:
- Check the mindset box when you have completed this day's cycle.
- To dive deeper, refer to chapter "The Value of the System."

Gratitude Reveals Growth

Week 3, Day 4 *(Traditionally Wednesday)*

TASK OF THE DAY (TOD)

Gratitude is a powerful choice we get to make each day. That is correct. It is 100 percent a choice. The amazing thing about gratitude is it is the only emotion that only we can choose to experience. I get that people say no one can make you happy or sad, but if you have lived life, you can understand that others can influence your feelings, no matter how "emotionally strong/shutoff" you are.

So, we know gratitude reveals growth, so let's spend time focusing on what we have to be grateful for. If you are in a bad situation, most people will focus on the problem at hand. If a tree falls on a house, there is a time to recognize the problem, but once it is recognized, we can either sit and stare at the tree on/in the house, or we can start looking for solutions.

Today, I want you to start being grateful no matter what. The best way to do this is to make a list of what you are grateful for, and anytime you feel that gratitude leaving your mind, review that list.

For the long term or any other problems you are dealing with that feel like they are "too much" for you, start reviewing what you have to be grateful for.

If a tree fell on your house and you are outside looking at it, you can be grateful that you are not under that tree.

Gratitude is a choice and is a state of mind that we can be in no matter what external factors influence our life. So let's be grateful for today and every day. If you lose the gratitude, just start back up again. Start reviewing what you have to be grateful for in your head or even out loud. Personally, I like to write it down. At first, it will feel like you are just going through the motions, but if you can do five minutes of reviewing and reflecting on what you are grateful for, you will not be able to avoid gratitude overtaking your emotions, and you will start seeing the options for growth in any situation.

Intentional Tips:
- Check the mindset box when you have completed this day's cycle.
- To dive deeper, refer to chapter "The Value of the System."

Track It: Follow-Through Is Difficult
Week 3, Day 5 *(Traditionally Thursday)*

TASK OF THE DAY (TOD)

Most people intend to do what they say they will do. We genuinely mean to get to it, and we feel bad when we don't do something. Because of that, we need to recognize that follow-through is difficult but not for the reason most people think. Following through on its own is as hard as the task we are trying to do, but the difficulty of the task is not what most of us struggle with when it comes to follow-through. The reason why following through is difficult is because we forget or lose focus on what we intended on doing.

Today, I want you to avoid follow-through. Here is how I want you to do it: when you say you will do something for the entire day, no matter who it is to or who it is with, write it down. Even if it is just you telling yourself you are going to do something today; we *must* write it down and do it.

On normal days, you would let things go, but today, you are going to make a list, and before you close your eyes to sleep, you will do what is on that task, schedule a specific time to do that task in the future, or delegate the task properly to someone else to do it.

Then, we will look at the list and reflect on how many things we say yes to in a day. How many things we may have forgotten we said yes to in a day. We offer ourselves to people when it is not needed and let them down. By letting them down, it is damaging the relationship. For today, you will follow-through on everything you say or be able to tell someone when it will get done and who it is who will do it.

Intentional Tips:
- Check the mindset box when you have completed this day's cycle.
- To dive deeper, refer to chapter "The Value of the System."

Write It: The Value Of Writing Things Down
Week 3, Day 6 *(Traditionally Friday)*

TASK OF THE DAY (TOD)

We started on this task yesterday, and it is so important that we need to "follow through" today and make sure it is something that is done not only internally but also externally. We should make sure that those who we are working with are seeing that we plan on following through on what we are doing.

This is like when you are at a restaurant, and the server takes a party of ten's order and says they do not need to write it down. Someone at the table always shakes their head with little to no faith that the order will come out right. You have a lot of people whom you are working with and because of that, continue writing down everything you say you are going to do, but make sure the people you are working with see it.

Keeping a piece of paper in your pocket is great to pull out. Using your phone is not ideal, as most people recognize phones as something that pulls attention away from the situation, but if you need to, just let them know you want to write down what you need to do.

Here is the most important part, just like yesterday, today, do not go to sleep unless you do the task, schedule specifically a date and time when you are going to do the task, or properly delegate someone else to do the task. This will increase the likelihood of your follow-through as well as the likelihood others are willing to follow you.

Intentional Tips:
- Check the mindset box when you have completed this day's cycle.
- To dive deeper, refer to chapter "The Value of the Planning."

No Obligation
Week 3, Day 7 *(Traditionally Saturday)*

TASK OF THE DAY (TOD)

As you are recognizing, we want to cherish our rest time and our downtime. We tended to spend a lot of time focusing on our obligations to the world and others. We are meant to be with people. We are meant to live with people. We are not meant to be obligated to anyone.

We have obligations that interfere with the life we are supposed to live. We let them control ourselves and our actions, and that stops today.

Today, choose not to give in to your artificial obligations. They are only in existence due to your choice. Yes, you have responsibilities but to feel obligated is a choice by only you. So for today, we are not going to allow obligations to get in our way of a restful fay. Get to them tomorrow, take care of them next week. But for today, you are only obligated to yourself. Tell your friends. Tell your family. Be with them. Be there for them but *be* for yourself.

It may sound difficult, but it is just because you haven't done it. We allow ourselves to be pulled by these obligations, so for today, release yourself and be yourself. You deserve it and have deserved it..

Intentional Tips:
- Check the mindset box when you have completed this day's cycle.
- To dive deeper, refer to chapter "The Value of the Choice."

WEEK 4

BE: *Finding Wisdom in the Life You Live*

Now you get to be what it is we are trying to teach. When you try to do it, it is easy to miss. When you become what you are trying to do, it is impossible to avoid. You will hear us talk about the value of "being," and this is where it starts. Be who you are, and live the life you are supposed to live.

This is when we need to make this system part of our life. As you go into the final week of the cycle, you have now Learned, Lived, and Understood what we are doing, and now it is time for you to just be.

This is where you will get the most out of this program as you make it your own and become what it is you are looking to do.

Stop talking and start being. One of my favorite things to remind myself of is I am a human being, not a human doing. Therefore, I need to stop all of the doing and start being.

Use The Wisdom You Learned Last Week
Week 4, Day 1 *(Traditionally Sunday)*

TASK OF THE DAY (TOD)

Wisdom is a word that is not used very often because it is not experienced as much these days. Now people confuse knowledge with wisdom, but wisdom is more than just information. We define wisdom as the use of the correct knowledge at the correct time in the correct way.

It is properly applying knowledge to an area of your life. We feel we need to search externally for wisdom, and we work with clients nearly every day to find the wisdom that we can pull from. Today, I want you to focus on picking something that happened last week and what you learned from it. Take the experience and learn from it. The next step is to take action based on the lesson you learned.

This is why our definition of wisdom is to use the correct knowledge at the correct time in the correct way. If we were to spend more time learning from our own experience versus waiting to be taught by others, we would be able to live a much easier life. As you plan your week this week, write down weekly wisdom that is based on something you learned last week that you plan on implementing this week.

Intentional Tips:
- Check the mindset box when you have completed this day's cycle.
- To dive deeper, refer to chapter "The Value of the System."

Learn Life To Live Life
Week 4, Day 2 *(Traditionally Monday)*

TASK OF THE DAY (TOD)

Yesterday you were suggested to find out what it is you experienced last week, learn from it, and try to implement it this week. Let's take this one another step further. Today, I want you to take that weekly wisdom that you created and live by it. Life shows us what we need to do and should be doing if we sit back, watch, listen, and learn from our experiences.

For the most part, we as humans don't listen. We don't listen to others, we don't listen to ourselves, and we definitely don't listen to our experiences. Some of us are better than others, but for the most part, we tend to disregard our experiences if the results are not long-term enough.

So let's continue the thought from yesterday. I want you to take the piece of wisdom you experienced and learned last week and create a plan for you to implement it each day this week. Starting with today, make sure you focus on the wisdom you created and think of ways to best implement it.

You have a lot of experience you can pull from, and imagine if you could never run out of wisdom. If we are the source of our own wisdom based on the experience we lived, we can start living life with fewer regrets.

Intentional Tips:
* Check the mindset box when you have completed this day's cycle.
* To dive deeper, refer to chapter "The Value of the Process."

Stop Doing All The Wrong Things For The Right Reasons

Week 4, Day 3 *(Traditionally Tuesday)*

TASK OF THE DAY (TOD)

We all want to live good lives. We want to make sure that we are doing the most with the time we have here. Because of that, a lot of us will do things right now that seem like they make sense to do, but in reality, they are hurting our chances of experiencing the life we want to live. We call this "doing the wrong things for the right reasons."

This is for the individuals who continuously sacrifice time with the family now, with the reasoning being it will allow us to spend more time with them later. Basically, I will work now so I can spend time with my family later. I am going to take this meeting so I can do X, Y, and Z later. When we see clients doing the wrong things for the right reasons, it is somewhat embarrassing for them when they recognize that they are saying no to what they want in the future today, so they can potentially experience it later.

In other words, I am sacrificing X now so I may be able to experience X in the future. I have people in my life that fortunately have opened my eyes to recognize that I can experience what I want in the future right now. I won't go on a vacation this year with my spouse, so I can spend my later life traveling with my spouse.

Now please understand, we get that sacrifices need to be made sometimes. All we are asking is for you to logically think through to make sure we are not doing the wrong things now for the right reasons later when we can experience what we want later, now. Instead, find a way to do it now.

For today, I want you to think of the life you want to live later and see what you can do now. If you want to spend your life traveling, fit in some travel now. If you want to spend time with your family, do it now. Think if you are waiting ten years to do it so you can do it "right" later. That is assuming that later is ever coming. Here is a thought, instead of saving up for one big vacation that might happen, let's do small ones throughout the ten years. Instead of waiting to spend time with your family, do it now.

Today, find ways to do what you want later now, just on a level that you can do right now. You will be able to experience what life has to offer, live a good life, and by following this concept in your life, you will be able to better live the exact life you want today and each day following.

Intentional Tips:
- Check the mindset box when you have completed this day's cycle.
- To dive deeper, refer to chapter "The Value of the System."

Manage Your Life The Way You Manage Your Job
Week 4, Day 4 *(Traditionally Wednesday)*

TASK OF THE DAY (TOD)

I was giving a talk outside of the United States, and anytime we teach internationally, I am always a bit concerned with what the culture will accept some of the things I say. Truths are constant, but application change and reception of information are different for everyone.

So I made this statement that if you manage your job the way you manage your life, you would be fired, and it offended people. Not even sure if it is people or a person, but if that offends you and you are reading it, let me apologize first, and secondly, tell you that you should manage your life better.

For today, I want you to do just that. Think about what you do to ensure you do your job well. Things like goal-setting, performance reviews, budgeting, conscious spending and time management, organized meetings, and communication. How are you doing that with your team members in your personal life? Your family, your friends, your community members?

Take the practices that you use in your work life and start using them in your personal life. Set goals, communicate well, manage your time, review your performance. These things work both inside of work and outside of work. Truth is constant; application changes. So apply what you do to succeed in work and use it in all areas of your life.

Intentional Tips:
- Check the mindset box when you have completed this day's cycle.
- To dive deeper, refer to chapter "The Value of the Choice."

Internal/Relational Widsom Experienced
Week 4, Day 5 *(Traditionally Thursday)*

TASK OF THE DAY (TOD)

As we wrap up this cycle, we are going to work on learning from our experiences. There is not much to read, but there is a lot to think about.

Today, I want you to think about how your internal and relational life is doing. Let's make sure we are setting the time this week to focus on this and also do something about it. This is why we do the Pulse Check in the LP. Did you give these two areas the time and attention needed for your life to be lived well? Think about these questions for some time this week.

Once we have spent the time we need to reflect on what we will need to do about it, we can then start to focus on what we are doing to move forward—schedule time to focus on these areas of your life. You may feel you are doing well in each area, but that does not mean that you should just go through the motions. Eventually, we find that life decays any foundation we build in these areas.

Stop now, review where you've been in these two areas, and then schedule times for you to work on these two areas in some way, shape, or form.

Intentional Tips:
- Check the mindset box when you have completed this day's cycle.
- To dive deeper, refer to chapter "The Value of the System."

Physical/Professional Wisdom Experienced
Week 4, Day 6 *(Traditionally Friday)*

TASK OF THE DAY (TOD)

Now that you have done your Internal and Relational tasks let's see what you will be doing for next week. As the week is coming to an end, you can think through what you are doing next week.

As you read yesterday, you know that we are looking to take care of our four vital signs. Because you just did this yesterday, there is little reason to write this out too much for you to read.

I want you to take time to reflect on how you did in your physical and professional life. Did you give it the attention and effort you feel it deserved?

Once you reflect on this, please now schedule the times throughout the week that you will dedicate to this. Schedule the Time Chunks where you will work on these tasks.

Enjoy the week of fulfillment next week, and get ready for a relaxing weekend!

Intentional Tips:
- Check the mindset box when you have completed this day's cycle.
- To dive deeper, refer to chapter "The Value of the System."

❏ Cycle 1 Mindset: <u>Mentee</u> *You are to do it as close as you can based on how I teach it.*	❏ Cycle 2 Mindset: <u>Peer</u> *You do it how you feel it needs to be done in your life.*	❏ Cycle 3 Mindset: <u>Mentor</u> *You think of how you can teach someone else how to do it.*

No Guilt: Choose Not To Act Due To Guilt
Week 4, Day 7 *(Traditionally Saturday)*

Task of the Day (TOD)

We act on guilt, but why? We should not be letting guilt dictate our lives, but yet we do—some more than others. But for today, on this day of relaxing, I need you to not allow guilt to control you.

No guilt; choose not to act due to guilt. Anytime you feel guilt, restructure that paradigm and focus on the true reason you feel that way. We can be triggered to act because this feeling comes over us, but before you act, you must remove the guilt.

We cannot allow guilt to dictate how we choose to act. We cannot allow ourselves to live this life that we did not choose and we do not want. So for today, you will live without guilt but acting by choice and not guilt.

Enjoy this relaxing day, and remember you will never need to act unless you choose to do so!

You're done, but this is just the beginning. Now start the next cycle or experience your new life!

Intentionality is the one thing most people feel they have, but few actually do. When I first started Life Pulse, I realized that the most consistent solution to most problems in people's lives is inputting intentionality. Our first tagline of the company was "bringing intentionality back to life," and it had two meanings.

The first is to revive intentionality. It has been nearly dismissed from our minds due to the instant gratification and lack of attention most things seem to need (although they still need it). The second is to bring it back to our lives personally. It is as if it has been missing.

Intentionality is the key to surviving. Humans have moved so far away from this natural state of mind. From the way we deal with stress to the way we focus on food. Intentionality has no part in the world of gluttony and "do what feels good now."

As you read in the book, I am all about you enjoying life, and that is why I feel intentionality is needed. Life is too short with no re-dos to just go through it like you're floating in a river. The current of life is rough, it is dangerous, and rarely do you experience a good outcome when you just let life dictate your actions.

At this time, assuming you made it through this book and all three cycles, it is not time to get started. **Live every ninety days with a consistent level of intentionality, and you will experience the exact life you want to live.** Help us bring intentionality back to life by introducing others to this concept. You can share the book, share the i90 challenge, or just be a walking example of what life looks like when it is lived with intention.

We are giving you the framework of how to live this life full of intention. It is not complicated, but it can be difficult. Although you need no more resources than this book and a pen, feel free to go to www.LifePulseInc. com to access all of the resources that we may refer to in this book. Enjoy what you are building; live the life you deserve to live. And enjoy the rest of your life you get to live with The Intentional Week.

Intentional Tips:
- Check the mindset box when you have completed this day's cycle.
- To dive deeper, refer to chapter "The Value of the Choice."

ABOUT THE AUTHOR

Matt Granados has been an entrepreneur since he was a teenager. Through his entrepreneurial journey, he built his first million-dollar business by the age of twenty-four. To develop his businesses, Matt focused on developing his people. While creating a sales organization reaching the $40 million mark in sales made up of individuals hired primarily from classified ads, Matt created a way to combine structure and intention, which allowed his "under-qualified" team to be the most effective, productive, and self-motivated versions of themselves.

This system was discovered by one of the largest financial institutions in the world, who asked Matt to share it with their team, as they felt it solved their biggest personal problem. They were finding it nearly impossible to connect their corporate desired metrics with their individuals' desired goals. In their eyes, Life Pulse's System does just that.

Although Matt has done this in multiple businesses of his own, it wasn't until this meeting that he recognized that the systems developed by Life Pulse could be used by individuals in businesses of all sizes. Since Matt created Life Pulse, Inc., the team and systems have worked with individuals and small businesses to the likes of Twitter, Google, and the United States Air Force.

Matt's first book, *Motivate the Unmotivated*, quickly became a number-one international bestseller and has launched Matt to be a sought-after expert on the ways of building sustainable motivation in teams and individuals, as well as teaching groups on how to experience intentional growth in all areas of business and life.

Matt lives outside of St. Louis, Missouri, with his amazing wife Maria and two amazing kids, Natalie (Nat G) and Zach (Zig). Out of all of the things he enjoys doing, *nothing* comes close to being the husband to his wife and the father for his kids. Everything he does leads back to them, and without them, none of this would be possible, and none of this would be worth it. Matt always knows content works when it passes his three tests. His experience, others' experience, and the hardest test to pass—does it work within my family? Matt believes that truth is constant and application changes, so anything that has truth should be able to withstand any part of life. Matt's family is his sounding board and the most important people in his life.